Thomas Austin

Religion and the New Majority

Religion and

BILLY GRAHAM, MIDDLE AMERICA,

the New Majority

AND THE POLITICS OF THE 70s

Lowell D. Streiker

AND

Gerald S. Strober

ASSOCIATION PRESS / NEW YORK

RELIGION AND THE NEW MAJORITY

Association Press, 291 Broadway, New York, N.Y. 10007

International Standard Book Number: 0-8096-1844-3
Library of Congress Catalog Card Number: 79-189009

Library of Congress Cataloging in Publication Data

Streiker, Lowell D.
Religion and the new majority.

Includes bibliographical references.
1. Graham, William Franklin, 1918– 2. U. S.—Religion—1945– 3. Fundamentalism. 4. U. S.—Politics and government—1969– I. Strober, Gerald S., joint author. II. Title.
BR515.S76 269'.2'0924 [B] 79-189009
ISBN 0-8096-1844-3

PRINTED IN THE UNITED STATES OF AMERICA

Contents

Prologue

Two friends were exchanging compliments. One man was the President of the United States. The other man was an Evangelist.

Said the Evangelist of the President:

"I have had the privilege and the opportunity of being with him privately in both victory and in defeat.

"I have seen him modest in victory and philosophical in defeat. I have watched him make many tough decisions that were right for America, though not always popular.

"I have seen his moral strength when the temptation was expediency and compromise. I remember once I made a suggestion to him. He looked at me and said, 'Billy, I don't think that would be morally right.'

"When I thought it through, I realized he was right. At that moment I felt that he was the preacher and I was the sinner." *

The President spoke of the decline of the great civilizations of antiquity—Persia, Greece, Rome. "They are dead," he declared, "because as they became wealthy they became soft. Without character and spirit and the moral strength of the people, a nation cannot survive." But elected officials, he continued, "cannot decree that a nation shall be morally or

* "Nixon and Evangelist Praise Each Other," Lawrence M. O'Rourke, Philadelphia *Evening Bulletin,* October 16, 1971, p. 1.

spiritually strong." † Such strength, the President insisted, depends on men like the Evangelist. He praised the Evangelist for inspiring the American people with a strong religious faith without which the nation cannot be great. "When the history of this time is written," the President concluded, the Evangelist may be credited with having performed "the most important works."

Two friends were exchanging compliments—one was Richard M. Nixon; the other, Billy Graham. The President and the Evangelist: the two men most admired by their fellow Middle Americans, the leaders of a constituency which comprises the new political majority; the priest of America's traditional religion and the king of America's civil religion, the only enduring heroes of Middle America.

The date was Friday, October 15, 1971. The place was Charlotte, North Carolina. The occasion: a tribute to the Charlotte-born Evangelist by tens of thousands who lined the streets and later crowded into Charlotte Coliseum. The President had come from Washington to this Piedmont plateau town with an entourage which included Mrs. Nixon, Secretary of the Treasury John Connally and his wife, the North Carolina congressional delegation, Mr. Nixon's personal friends Bebe Rebozo and Hobart Lewis, the latter chairman of the board of *Reader's Digest,* and South Carolina Senator J. Strom Thurmond.

Page One headlines proclaimed "NIXON AND EVANGELIST PRAISE EACH OTHER," while a photograph of four smiling participants (Graham, Mrs. Graham, North Carolina Governor Bob Scott, and Nixon) momentarily forced the Vietnamese War, the economy, racial strife, crime, and local politics from the center of public attention. When the history of our time is written, this meeting of friends may well be remembered not merely as the day in which an American President unveiled a plaque marking an Evangelist's birthplace, but also as a reaffirmation of the religious convictions without which the America of Richard M. Nixon and the

† *Ibid.*

America of Billy Graham would disappear from the center of history.

This book is about America's new political majority, its faith, and its leaders. It is an account of the religion of Middle America and the ways in which this religion will influence the political decisions made by Americans in the perilous days ahead.

We are indebted to Miss Lillian Block for making available library materials from Religious News Service; Dr. Robert Ferm and Dr. T. W. Wilson extended helpful cooperation on behalf of the Billy Graham Evangelistic Association.

1

The Mood of Middle America

"We are proud of ourselves, that's what I'd like to say. We're not sure of things, though; we're uncertain, I'm afraid, and when you're like that—worried, that is—then you're going to lose a little respect for yourself. You're not so proud any more." [1] Proud and uncertain—this is the voice of Middle America.

Who are the Middle Americans? One observer uses the term in "its admittedly imprecise but generally accepted sense: the large body of working-class citizens, members of families conveniently labeled blue collar, lower middle and middle income, on the whole not college educated, old enough to remember the economic insecurity of the Depression." [2] Another observer finds it easier to explain what Middle Americans are *not*: "They are not black, not red, not brown, not unemployed, not eligible for or desirous of welfare, not intellectuals, not hippies, not members of a drug scene, a youth cult, a 'counterculture,' not in general against our military position in the world, not rich, not professional men, not 'big business,' not individuals exceptionally well-born, well-to-do, well-educated—well able to influence their communities this way or that." [3]

They are the one hundred and thirty million Americans who are caught in the middle. "Let's face it," says Saul

Alinsky, caustically tough radical activist. "The middle class represents four-fifths of this country's population. If you took every minority group in this country and somehow got them together, they still wouldn't have the numbers to change things. The middle class has the numbers, but they feel too cut off from the entire society to change things. Someone has got to show them how to get a voice in this country." [4]

Though proud and uncertain, vehement and bitter, Middle America is not silent. Karl Fleming says of his trip through Middle America: "People seemed almost pathetically eager to talk, as if nobody had ever asked before, and almost universally they were in a fretful, fearful, disquieted mood." Things are not the way they ought to be, not the way they used to be, not the way I was taught they should be—such is the feeling of Middle America. Everything has changed and none of the rules, values, and standards of an earlier America applies any longer. According to Richard Lemon, it is easy to catalogue the changes that the Middle American does not like:

> The middle American was brought up to respect hard work; now millions are being given money for doing nothing, and affluent youngsters are announcing that work is nonsense. He was taught to behave well; now thousands of rebels shout filthy insults even at policemen. . . . He always held to a strict code of public morality; now he can hardly walk down the street without seeing nudity and sex advertised. He was taught that children obeyed their parents; now they don't obey anybody. He was taught that drugs were used only by the debased; marijuana and much stronger drugs are now available almost everywhere. He thought the church was supposed to be a sanctuary of righteousness; now priests and ministers take to the streets to demonstrate for causes he doesn't believe in. He thought that the flag was sacred and patriotism was a virtue; today, the flag is dragged and burned, millions protest against a war, and the term "super patriot" is one of scorn. He thought that Negroes were beneath him, whether they deserved to be or not; now he thinks they are getting favors denied to him. . . . He thought that owning your own car and house and minding

your own business was a worthy goal; now he has reached it, and he finds himself ridiculed by young people and intellectuals. . . .

He always respected technology, and now it is befouling his air and his lakes. He expected technological systems to work, and they break down. He thought the country was enormous, and it suddenly seems to be jammed full of people. He thought that Americans could handle anything, and now mayors of great cities call them ungovernable and the country is lost in a war it can't seem to end.[5]

THE GROWTH OF PESSIMISM

There has been an erosion of confidence in the ability of America to solve either national or international problems. The situation we confront today is not unlike the one we faced twenty years ago. As Robert Roth reports:

We had a war in Asia then—as we have now—and we had a candidate for President who ran on the promise that he would end the war, and did—six months after he took office.

We had large pockets of uneasiness then. It was the day of compulsory loyalty oaths, and of people hounded out of jobs on charges of disloyalty made by faceless accusers. But at its worst the fever afflicted only a small percentage of the population.

Now we have an entire country involved in antagonisms—white against black, old against young, city against suburb, conformists against dissenters, and we have seen the flames of mass animosity fanned not just by one spectacular senator [the late Joseph R. McCarthy of Wisconsin] but by a President, a Vice President, an attorney general, almost an entire Administration, which sought to win election by persuading people that their chief problem was crime and that the way to deal with it was, in Mr. Nixon's phrase, to put an end to the "creeping permissiveness" in the home, the school and the courts.[6]

But what most distinguishes the Nixon from the Eisenhower era is the current lack of confidence in our ability to solve the problems that beset us. A mood of uncertainty has spread over the land. The headlines of our daily newspapers yield, in the words of Robert B. Semple, Jr., "a portrait of a nation confused." Semple elaborates:

> One turns the pages of the daily newspapers in vain search for some shred of agreement, reconciliation, continuity. But the reports are reports of a people who are at worst mean-tempered and at best vaguely uneasy about distant forces over which they exercise diminishing control.[7]

Twenty years ago, few doubted that the war would end, that our national problems would somehow be solved, that the government could be trusted. But today, all of these things are doubted by many Americans. As Roth maintains, "This presents a problem more serious than any faced in the McCarthy era. For no national problem can be solved unless there first exists a national belief that the solution is within the national grasp."[8]

A survey designed by Potomac Associates finds that almost half the American population fears that the country is beset by unrest "serious enough to lead to a real breakdown." Fifty-seven per cent of those between the ages of 21 and 29, and 51 per cent of those between the ages of 30 and 49 share this pessimistic outlook. The only group which seems reasonably sure that present unrest is "likely to blow over soon" are those 50 and over. Republicans and those Americans with no more than a grade-school education, however, were slightly more inclined to optimism. The following table indicates the percentage of Americans choosing each response.

AMERICANS' FEELING ABOUT CURRENT UNREST[9]

	Will Lead to Breakdown %	*Will Blow Over* %	*Can't Say* %
NATIONAL AVERAGE	47	38	15
AGE			
21–29	57	30	13
30–49	51	35	14
50 & over	37	45	18

EDUCATION			
College	49	34	17
High school	49	39	12
Grade school	38	41	21
INCOME			
Upper	45	40	15
Upper middle	49	39	12
Lower middle	48	37	15
Lower	41	38	21
POLITICAL AFFILIATION			
Democrat	45	37	18
Republican	42	45	13
Independent	53	35	12

Even those who approve of the way President Nixon has been doing his job are split on whether or not current unrest is serious enough to lead to a real breakdown (43 per cent fear a breakdown; 44 per cent do not; 13 per cent have no opinion). Those who *disapprove* of the President's performance are convinced of a possible breakdown (54 per cent to 33 per cent; 13 per cent undecided).

When the Cantril-Roll study is compared with similar surveys conducted in 1959 and 1964, it becomes apparent that the American citizen's hopes and fears for his nation have undergone considerable transformation. Americans are less concerned with material prosperity, international cooperation, and the threat of war, and more concerned with national unity, law and order, and the environment. The following table indicates the percentage of Americans listing each particular hope and fear for the nation.

HOPES AND FEARS FOR NATION [10]

National Hopes	1959 %	1964 %	1971 %
Peace	48	51	51
Economic stability; no inflation	12	5	18
Employment	13	15	16
National unity	1	9	15
Law and order	3	4	11
Better standard of living	20	28	11
Solution of pollution problems	—	—	10
Settlement of racial problems	14	15	10
Improved public morality	7	10	8
International cooperation; reduced tensions	17	6	7
Solution of drug problem	—	—	6

National Fears	1959 %	1964 %	1971 %
War (esp. nuclear war)	64	50	30
National disunity; political instability	3	8	26
Economic instability; inflation	18	13	17
Communism	12	29	12
Lack of law and order	3	5	11
Pollution	—	—	9
Drugs	—	—	7
Racial tensions	—	9	7
Unemployment	7	6	7
Lack of public morality	4	5	6
Loss of personal freedom	4	5	5

A further indication of the increase in pessimism is found in the decline of those who regard the settlement of racial problems a national hope (14 per cent in 1959; 10 per cent in 1971) during a period in which racial tensions, drugs, and pollution have been added to the list of national fears. Although we are not nearly so frightened by the prospect of war as we once were, we seem to be a good deal more afraid of our neighbors, our society, and our environment.

As a nation we continue to believe in the American Way of Life—the importance of the family, the need to work hard in order to obtain the benefits of the good life, the sanctity of private property, the freedom to pursue comfort, security, and pleasure. What enormous economic strides most of us have made in the past four decades!

How, then, has the dream become a nightmare? For the United States of America, the strongest and wealthiest nation in the history of mankind, is a land of poisoned air and polluted water, of racial strife and rampant crime, of personal instability and interpersonal alienation, of ulcers and divorce. Americans as a people are beset by skyrocketing expectations, hopeless dreams, and insatiable appetites. For the foundations of their lives are the advertisers' hollow promises of eternal youth, instant success, and sexual irresistibility—all for the price of a pack of cigarettes, a tube of toothpaste, a can of deodorant or a bottle of mouthwash.

But listen to the responses of Americans under thirty. According to the same Potomac Associates survey only 30 per cent are convinced that current unrest will blow over. More than half believe that America is headed for a major breakdown. What has happened to the children of the American dream—the well-fed, well-housed, well-schooled makers of our tomorrow and disturbers of our today? The late Robert F. Kennedy heaped accolades upon them. "Not since the founding of the Republic," he declared, "has there been a younger generation of Americans brighter, better educated, more highly motivated than this one." [11] He praised them for "an idealism and a devotion to country matched in few nations, and excelled in none." [12] In his inaugural address, President Richard M. Nixon echoed this sentiment:

> We see the hope of tomorrow in the youth of today. I know America's youth. I believe in them. We can be proud that they are better educated, more committed, more passionately driven by conscience than any generation in our history.

Yet implicit in these celebrations of the passion and idealism of today's younger generation is the recognition that the usually stable albeit tense relationship between the young and their elders has been severely shaken. The young find themselves alienated from their parents' world and value structure. Young Americans are discovering that "in the industrial West, and increasingly now in the uncommitted nations, ardor is lacking: instead men talk of their growing distance from each other, from their social order, from their work and play, and from the values and heroes which in a perhaps romanticized past seem to have given order, meaning, and coherence to their lives." [13] As Eldridge Cleaver eloquently observes, "It is among the white youth of the world that the greatest change is taking place. It is they who are experiencing the great psychic pain of waking into consciousness to find their inherited heroes turned by events into villains." [14]

Today's adults show the most irrational hostility toward their own offspring. Public support of the National Guardsmen who shot the students at Kent State was overwhelming—

80 per cent of adults polled approved of the shooting before any of the circumstances were known. Perhaps Cleaver is correct, and "the traditional tolerance which every older generation has found it necessary to display is . . . exhausted, leaving a gulf of fear, hostility, mutual misunderstanding, and contempt."[15]

But what of the other side of the "generation gap"? How does the current young American regard his elders. According to many observers, today's adults have been radically "de-authoritized" in the eyes of their sons and daughters. In the words of Robert Paul Wolff:

> America has lost no wars; it has suffered no depressions. The generation of the fathers has achieved an unbroken chain of material successes for almost 30 years. If the failure is neither *military* nor *economic,* we can only conclude that it is essentially *moral.* Listen to the voices of the students. They accuse the fathers of the very crimes that the fathers lay at the door of Nazi Germany and Communist Russia: racism, genocide, imperialism, aggression, authoritarian manipulation of subject populations for selfish and evil ends.[16]

"OURS IS AN AGE . . . OF ALIENATION"

An apocalyptical mood prevails. Observers of the social and political scene, the state of the environment, and international affairs seem to vie with one another for the honor of delivering the gloomiest prognosis. Things are getting worse, they tell us. And the worse things get, the more jubilant the now vindicated forecasters seem to become. One wonders if we are not cursed with self-fulfilling prophecies. The worse things get, the worse we expect them to become. And the worse we expect them to become, the worse they will surely get. As Keniston laments:

> The prevailing images of our culture are images of disintegration, decay and despair; our highest art involves the fragmentations and distortion of traditional realities; our best drama depicts suffering, misunderstanding and breakdown; our worthiest novels are narratives of loneliness, searching, and

> unfulfillment; even our best music is, by earlier standards, dissonant, discordant and inhuman. Judged by the values of past generations, our culture seems obsessed with breakdown, splintering, disintegration and destruction. Ours is an age not of synthesis but of analysis, not of constructive hopes but of awful destructive potentials, not of commitment, but of alienation.[17]

Even the President of the United States voices the fear that we have lost our national will to greatness. Speaking to Midwest news editors in Kansas City, President Nixon said:

> What has happened . . . is that great civilizations of the past, as they have become wealthy, as they have lost their will to live, to improve, they then have become subject to the decadence that eventually destroys the civilization. The United States is now reaching that period.[18]

THE RESISTANCE OF MIDDLE AMERICA TO CHANGING RELIGIOUS VALUES

What do these proud and uncertain Americans believe? What is their relationship to the churches of America? From what sources other than the churches do they receive confirmation of the way in which they experience reality? What is the religion of Middle America? What are their basic convictions, and how do their beliefs influence the way they vote, the way they think, the way they live? Lutz is convinced that "to a large extent those Middle Americans are the persons who populate the rolls of our churches, who give money (increasingly less these days) to support national denominational or ecumenical programs, who respond more like rebellious donkeys than like passive sheep to the leadership of activist shepherds." Middle Americans, he maintains, "are exceedingly uptight about social change . . . increasingly angry about what they see as an alliance between establishment elitists and alienated rich kids, minorities and poor people." In sum, they are "dumbfounded at what they consider an abrupt rewriting of a value system they were taught was Christian, with their own church leaders taking an eager part in the rewriting job." [19]

"I haven't given the church a penny in two years," says a workingman in Milwaukee. "They're supposed to teach kids to love thy neighbor, not all this racial stuff. I despise them now. If they want to bury me in the Catholic church, fine. If not, tough." [20]

A young priest sent to preach one Sunday in a white parish in New Orleans interpreted "love thy neighbor" to mean that whites and blacks should accept one another in an integrated society. A worshiper stood up in the middle of the congregation and shouted: "I didn't come here to listen to this kind of junk, I came to hear mass." More than fifty people angrily stormed out of the church. "If I miss mass today, *it's your fault,*" one of them shouted at the priest.[21]

"I used to go to church and the preacher would talk about God, Jesus, and the Bible," said a man in Minneapolis. "Now he tells me why I shouldn't buy grapes." [22] When the Archdiocese of Detroit pledged one million dollars for the aid of the poor and minority groups, many Catholics withheld their contributions to the Church. When the 183rd General Assembly of the United Presbyterian Church, U.S.A., voted to give ten thousand dollars to the Angela Davis defense fund, their nationwide constituency overwhelmingly denounced this action.

If these reactions to the churches are representative of Middle America, then the institutions of American religion have failed to prepare their constituencies for the personal, social, and political challenges of the Seventies. The churches are not alone, however, in their inability to offer remedies for dealing with America's present mood of uncertainty. Virtually every institution of American life has proved itself inadequate. "If a way is found," remarks Lemon, "it probably will be by applying the old spirit which most Americans cherish to the new problems which they have come to fear." [23] But what is this "old spirit" and how can it inspire us in an age of revolutionary changes? As we shall explain in the following pages, the answer is not simple. For the religion of Middle America weaves together three strands: 1) the personal piety of revivalistic fundamentalism, 2) the myths and symbols of American civil religion, and 3) the liberal-humanist heritage. At present all three traditions are responding in novel ways to the challenges of the nation's socio-political circumstances. We have attempted to discern these responses and to predict the manner in which they will influence America in the perilous days ahead. It is our contention that America is a religious nation, and that the religion of its people is alive and well and active and effective despite the confusion of the times. Further, we are convinced that at the very center of the religious response to the crisis of the present stands Billy Graham, whose charismatic, priestly, and prophetic leadership commands an ever-increasing number of Americans and whose role in American life is of decisive significance for our national future.

NOTES

1. Robert Coles, *The Middle Americans, Proud and Uncertain* (Boston: Little, Brown and Company, An Atlantic Monthly Press Book, 1971), p. 3.
2. Charles P. Lutz, "Middle America: Theologically Formed," *Christian Century,* March 18, 1970, p. 323.
3. Coles, *op. cit.,* p. v.
4. Quoted by Richard Lemon, *The Troubled Majority* (New York: Simon and Schuster, 1970), p. 19.
5. *Ibid.,* pp. 46–47.
6. Philadelphia *Sunday Bulletin,* February 14, 1971, Section 2, News and Views, p. 1.
7. New York *Times,* Sunday, September 28, 1969, Section 4, The Week in Review, p. 1.
8. Philadelphia *Sunday Bulletin,* February 14, 1971, Section 2, News and Views.
9. Albert H. Cantril and Charles W. Roll, Jr., *Hopes and Fears of the American People,* as reported by Nancy Greenberg, "The Agony Within America," in the Philadelphia *Sunday Bulletin,* August 8, 1971, Section 2, News and Views, pp. 1 and 6.
10. *Ibid.*
11. *To Seek a Newer World* (New York: Bantam Books, 1968), p. 1.
12. *Ibid.*
13. Kenneth Keniston, *The Uncommitted: Alienated Youth in American Society* (New York: Harcourt, Brace & World, Inc., 1965), p. 3.
14. *Soul on Ice* (New York: Dell Publishing Co., Inc., 1968), p. 69.

15. *Ibid.*, p. 70.
16. Review of *The Conflict of Generations* by Lewis S. Feuer, *The New York Times Book Review*, March 30, 1969, p. 32.
17. Keniston, *op. cit.*, p. 4.
18. *Time* Magazine, July 19, 1971, p. 8.
19. *Ibid.*
20. Quoted by Richard Lemon, *op. cit.*, p. 59.
21. Thomas Merton, *Conjectures of a Guilty Bystander* (New York: Doubleday Image Books, 1966), pp. 343–344.
22. Cited by Lemon, *op. cit.*, p. 59.
23. *Ibid.*, p. 218.

2

Billy Graham—Prophet, Priest, and Quintessential Middle American

For eleven months of the year Pasadena lies sleepily at the foot of the San Gabriel Mountains, a lovely city of pastel homes, well-manicured lawns and wide avenues. Only when one turns westward to the freeway which leads to Los Angeles does the normal workday world seem to intrude on the town which otherwise makes up another bedroom community outside the City of Angels. But in December all this changes and at the end of the month Pasadena explodes. At the Sheraton, on Colorado Boulevard—the main drag—and in shops, schools and the city college, conversation begins and ends with two significant pieces of Americana, the Tournament of Roses parade and the Rose Bowl football game.

Late in the month thousands of visitors carrying signs made in McKeesport, Pa., Ottumwa, Iowa, and Longwood, Colo., arrive, their ranks then swelled by Angelinos, Valleyites and finally Pasadenans happy to share their city with a genuine cross section of Middle America. Twenty-four hours before the first marching unit steps off from South Orange Grove Boulevard the sidewalks are littered with tents, sleeping bags, chairs, and much of the other equipment Americans on the move take to whatever sites their trailers and campers carry them. Status on the morrow will be severely stratified according to whether one has a ticket to the parade or the game, or—wonder of wonders—ducats for both. And great events they are—witness the TV mobile units, the newspaper linage, and the more than two million people who jam into Pasadena on January 1.

Sitting in the stands, feeling the warm winter sun, listening to the bands, watching as floats representing Ford, Holiday Inn and dozens of other familiarly known brand names move by, one realizes that this is America, at its corniest, yes, in campiest drag, yes; but in a rather profound sense it is also the America that motivates and represents decision-making whether it be in Detroit, Pittsburgh, Washington or Wall Street—a microcosm of the larger stage where the real American will please stand up.

BILLY GRAHAM: THE MAN AND THE SYMBOL

And on New Year's Day 1971 who should lead the Tournament of Roses Parade, riding gloriously in the powder-blue convertible which once displayed Ike, Bob Hope, the twelve Apollo astronauts, Walt Disney, and the homegrown Californian, Richard Nixon? Billy Graham, the first clergyman in the history of the parade to act as Grand Marshal! Billy Graham, chosen as "a symbol of hope, peace, and renewed faith in God and a world recognized leader as well as a friend of mankind." [1] Deeply tanned and relaxed after two weeks in Southern California, Graham smiled, waved to the crowd, and several times during the two-mile run down Colorado Boulevard extended his forefinger skyward indicating allegiance to Christ, in the "one-way" sign currently popular among Christian youth.

As the Cadillac made its slow way between the grandstands Graham's comment in accepting the role of Grand Marshal seemed highly applicable. Speaking in Pasadena at a news conference on September 29, 1970 he said "The

Tournament Committee may be saying to the world it is time the world looked to God and the Church for the answers to our problems. . . . We are in a pluralistic society; I think I'm representative of Jews and many Christians who worship God." [2] Graham leading the Rose Parade indeed represented the coming together of religion and Middle America, the fusing of traditional American values and contemporary attitudinal fashion, the great center of American mores and life thus symbolized in the person of the second-most-admired individual in the United States.[3]

As Billy and Ruth Graham rode past the cheering throng they must have reflected upon the long path traversed since Wheaton College days when Billy had joined a fellow classmate in moving furniture to help pay tuition. In a genuine sense the Rose Parade was not only a celebration of American life but also a celebration of one particular American life, a joyous acknowledgment of a success story, the upward movement of a man from farm to small-town college to suburban pastorate to national recognition and international acclaim.

BILLY GRAHAM: A SUMMARY OF HIS CAREER

The path to leadership began on a farm at Charlotte, N.C., on November 7, 1918. William Franklin Graham, Jr. was the first child born to Frank and Morrow Graham, doctrinally strict Scotch Presbyterians who tended, however, to be moderate in their handling of their son who, contrary to his mother's prayers, aspired to be a baseball player rather than a minister.

The early years were filled with experiences common to the region which was just coming to grips with the twentieth century and young Graham was responsible for pulling his weight on the farm, milking cows and working in the fields. During this period Graham was influenced not only by his parents and his environment, but also by Reese Brown, the Negro foreman, a former Army sergeant whom Billy would describe in later years as "one of the strongest men I ever saw. He had a tremendous capacity for work and great intelligence. He had a profound effect upon my life in its earliest years."[4]

At the age of sixteen Graham underwent a religious crisis not uncommon to Southern youngsters who lived in an atmosphere permeated by the outer trappings of the old-time religion. Graham's moment occurred when Mordecai Ham, a reasonably well-known evangelist, came to Charlotte for a series of meetings sponsored by friends of the Graham family. After attending several meetings Billy gave his heart to Christ and was saved. Also influenced by Ham during this period were the brothers Grady and T. W. Wilson, who became lifelong friends and associates of Graham.

The three young men enrolled at Bob Jones College in Cleveland, Tennessee, where the fiery evangelist of the 1920's had retired to develop a training school for Christian workers. Graham found the Jones educational philosophy to be harsh and unforgiving and after one year he left to continue his studies at the Florida Bible Institute at Tampa. Here his decision was made to enter the ministry and here also he evidenced for the first time the powers of preaching which would take him across the nation and world. Upon graduation Graham, sensing the need for further training, particularly in secular subjects, went up to Wheaton College in Illinois, then as now one of the most respected evangelical colleges in the country.

At Wheaton, Graham found a life partner, the daughter of a medical missionary, Ruth Bell. Ruth, born and raised in China, had, according to the judgment of her housemother, "the most beautiful Christian character of any young person I have ever known. She has the intellectual qualities to make a success in any work she would choose to undertake."[5] Ruth's father, Dr. L. Nelson Bell, was to play an increasingly important role in Billy's career. Bell, a lifelong Presbyterian, widened Graham's appreciation for the status of Christian faith within the major denominations thereby saving him from the narrowness to which many of his Wheaton contemporaries fell prey.

In 1943 Graham graduated with a degree in anthropology and looked forward to being pastor at the Village Baptist Church in nearby Western Springs as well as taking up graduate studies at the University of Chicago. If all went as planned he would enter the Army chaplaincy the following year. Early in his new pastorate Graham received a request from Torrey Johnson, a well-known local minister and professor of New Testament at Northern Baptist Seminary, to take over a weekly religious broadcast. The program, *Songs in the Night,* heard in the Chicago area had become a burden to Johnson who was busy developing plans which would lead to the formation of an organization to be known as Youth for Christ.

Graham convinced his skeptical church leadership to underwrite the program and within a matter of weeks the broadcast became self-sustaining, eventually reaching into eighteen states. Soon after Graham started his responsibilities on *Songs in the Night,* Johnson was after him again, this time to help in the building of Youth for Christ. On May 20, 1944, Graham spoke to his first large audience in Orchestra Hall, Chicago. The sermon was preceded by "the worst fit of stage fright in my life." [6] Forty-two young persons responded to the invitation for commitment to Christ.

Evangelism: The Early Years

Convinced that Graham was the man who could extend his new organization into a national movement, Johnson persuaded him to resign his pastorate and chaplaincy commission to travel the country for Youth for Christ. Graham's decision, facilitated by a severe case of the mumps which destined his Army service to be limited to desk activity, marked a watershed in his life. His work with Youth for Christ would take him in the next few years to every major city in the United States and many foreign centers as well as put him in contact with the men who were to form the nucleus of his future evangelistic organization. By 1948 Graham had put together a team of co-workers to hold evangelistic rallies in major population areas. In the same year he accepted the presidency of Northwestern Schools, a Bible college in Minneapolis which had been founded by one of the leading Midwest fundamentalists, William B. Riley. Graham left the business management of the college in the capable hands of George Wilson and continued his travels.

In September 1949 the single most important series of meetings of his career began in Los Angeles. Graham, together with his team of old friend and associate evangelist Grady Wilson, song leader Cliff Barrows, and soloist George Beverly Shea, intended to conduct a three-week campaign in a tent just outside the downtown business district. Just prior to the Los Angeles meetings Graham underwent a dark night of the soul in which his faith was tried largely through growing doubts about the veracity of the Scriptures as articulated by his close friend and colleague, Charles Templeton. After a particularly difficult session in which Graham was criticized for his view of biblical interpretation, he devoted himself to an extensive study of biblical passages concerning authority. He became convinced of the trustworthiness of Scripture and accepted "this Book by faith as the Word of God." [7]

In Los Angeles a series of sensational conversions involving a cowboy singer, an ex-Olympic athlete, and a wiretapper for the crime syndicate brought the campaign widespread media attention. But the most important incident in Los Angeles was the message flashed by William Randolph Hearst to his editors across the country to "puff Graham." Hearst, evidently hearing of Graham from a household employee and impressed by the evangelist's message, was thus responsible for nationwide attention being focused on Graham.[8] The original three-week commitment stretched to fourteen weeks and led Billy to conclude "the work has been God's and not man's. I want no credit or glory. I want the Lord Jesus to have it all." [9]

Invitations to hold campaigns soon poured in from major cities across the country. Graham moved next to Boston to honor a commitment made in 1947. Working in close relationship with Harold John Ockenga,[10] minister of the historic Park Street Church and then as in the years to follow a close advisor, Graham early in January 1950 repeated the Los Angeles triumph, climaxing his activity by preaching to sixteen thousand persons in Boston Garden, January 16. He then moved to Columbia, S.C., for a series of meetings which featured the appearance of the governor on the platform [11] and a late-night meeting with Henry Luce at the estate of Bernard Baruch.

It was in Columbia that Graham added Willis Haymaker to his staff. Haymaker, who had directed organization for evangelists Gypsy Smith and Bob Jones, came up with the term "Crusade" to describe Graham's efforts. John Pollock tells us that soon after Graham was speaking of "a crusade to bring America to her knees in repentance of sin and faith toward God." [12] This marked a deepening of Graham's ministry as he sensed the implications of a nationwide movement toward individual salvation.

The Evangelist as a National Figure

By 1950 Graham had become a national personality and on July 14 he was invited to the White House to meet President Truman. This conference was the forerunner of many conversations he would have with Presidents in the executive mansion. America at this point was moving into a new phase of the postwar religious revival. In the years immediately following the war the desire to obtain new and better consumer goods was coupled by an inner need to make sense out of the heritage of national disruption and personal confusion which had been left by the experience of global conflict. Books such as *Peace of Mind, Peace of Soul* and Norman Vincent Peale's *The Power of Positive Thinking* [13] directed the way toward the restoration of inner tranquility and told Americans how they could build new lives in the postwar world. The message of these works and others stressed man and God in co-operation to build better, happier persons in a new world of peace. Events, however, interrupted the group honeymoon; by the early 1950's the grim reality was a world troubled by tensions and once more on the brink of conflict. Obviously something more than a cooperative relationship between man and God was needed. More radical transformation of the personal and national psyche was called for and it was into this breach that the evangelistic message of Billy Graham was directed. Americans living with the threat of atomic holocaust were told that individual and national redemption could occur only when men realized their inadequacy, their sins, their inability to change either themselves or the world in which they lived. They must turn completely, wholly, to Christ who would forgive their sins, make them new creations and fill them with his spirit. With this new strength they might conquer inner problems even as they were focusing their efforts at national amelioration through evangelism. The evangelistic message so central to Graham's ministry was similar to that of the great revivalists Moody and Sunday, but Graham was to build a larger, more inclusive and longer-lasting constituency than these earlier evangelists.

Growth of the Graham Constituency

At the moment Graham ascended to national stature he assumed leadership of the burgeoning neo-evangelical movement which developed in the forties around a circle of sophisticated theological conservatives led by the seminary professors, Carl F. H. Henry and Edward John Carnell.[14] This movement stressed the fundamentals of faith as articulated in the famous modernist-fundamentalist controversy of the 1920's, but its theological principles were formulated with considerable intellectual acumen and integrity. In addition Henry and Carnell stressed the need for Christians to understand the economic, social and political currents active in American life. Neo-evangelicalism posed a serious challenge to the liberalism which survived the two wars. By the time the National Council of Churches was organized in 1950 this new fundamentalism was gaining adherents and stood ready to do battle largely through its organizational arm, the National Association of Evangelicals (NAE), a loose confederation of smaller denominations and individual churches. By identifying with neo-evangelicalism and the NAE, Graham firmly moved his ministry from the constricted channels of the older fundamentalism of Jones, John R. Rice and Carl McIntire, while at the same time he placed himself at the head of those forces which would gain in strength over the next two decades as the NCC and the major denominations fell into disfavor with significant blocks of constituents.

In 1950 Graham took two steps which would consolidate and solidify his status as an evangelical leader and national personality. On November 5 he launched the Hour of Decision radio broadcast, heard initially over 125 stations. Later in the month as a device to handle the inquiries and finances related to the program as well as to administer the growing crusade schedule, the Billy Graham Evangelistic Association was incorporated as a nonprofit entity. Graham, realizing he could not give day-by-day attention to the Association's activities, appointed George Wilson, his Northwestern Schools' business manager to be secretary-treasurer. Wilson, an able and aggressive businessman with an appreciation of advances in technology, quickly set up the framework of what has become one of the most efficient and successful national religious organizations. In 1970 income exceeding fifteen million dollars flowed into the Association's Minneapolis headquarters in response to radio and television solicitations as well as in payment and rental fees for books and films. To those who wonder how the funds are disbursed and question the ethical and practical effects this huge income has on Graham and his associates, the answer given by John Corry in *Harper's* is sufficient: "For years . . . snoopy reporters have tried to find evidence that someone in the Graham organization was stealing money or at least making too much of it. No one has found the evidence and it is just as well to let the thought die." [15] Suffice to add that Graham, whose current salary is $24,500, is as scrupulously honest in his financial

organization, perhaps the most significant activities of the period were related to Graham's response to the many social and political crises of the 1960's. Birmingham, Watts, Newark, Vietnam, the youth revolution, and especially the 1968 election would affect Graham the evangelist and Graham the public personality far more than the crusade schedule or its results.

The Evangelist as an Ecumenical Figure

Interestingly, Graham in the late sixties became a significant ecumenical figure, not as might be imagined simply within the confines of Protestantism, but among Roman Catholics and Jews as well. In July of 1968 Bishop John Wright of Pittsburgh called upon Catholic clergy and laity in his diocese to pray for the upcoming Graham crusade. Wright, who now holds a key theological post in the Roman Curia said, "Even those who do not share other elements of the crusade theology rejoice that a powerful voice will be lifted in Pittsburgh to proclaim the divinity of our Saviour Jesus Christ." [18] Three months later the editor of the Catholic monthly *The Lamp,* Rev. Charles Angell, praised Graham for his "updated appeal to the whole man." Later, in an interview with Religious News Service, Father Angell cited Graham for "unqualified dedication, total sincerity, charismatic appeal and relevant preaching." [19]

Graham's relationship with the Jewish community was greatly strengthened with the release in March 1970 of the World Wide Pictures film, *His Land,* a beautifully made and moving articulation of Graham's theological understanding of the State of Israel. The film, which by the next fall had been screened in churches throughout the United States and Canada, was hailed by Jewish leaders as perhaps the finest Christian statement on Israel since the birth of the state in May, 1948. Rabbi Marc H. Tanenbaum, national inter-religious affairs director of the American Jewish Committee, stated that the film, "communicates in dramatic, warmly sympathetic terms, a moving documentary which communicates the humanity and living reality of the Jewish people, their struggles and achievements in Israel." [20] Soon after, Tanenbaum added, "For acts of friendship toward the Jewish people at a time of turmoil which has not been altogether congenial to Jewish security, Billy Graham deserves better than a stereotyped skeptical response from thoughtful Jews and many others, while not ignoring basic differences." [21] One year later Graham reacted strongly to the trials of Soviet Jews then taking place in Riga, Latvian S.S.R. In a statement released from Minneapolis he called upon Christians to "join in prayer for the Riga defendants." Graham further stated, "I am deeply concerned and disturbed about the plight of Soviet Jews, some of whom have been imprisoned and held incommunicado. Apparently their only crime is that they are Jewish." [22] Roy Larson, religion editor of the Chicago *Sun-Times,* acknowledged Graham's contribution to Christian-Jewish understanding when he wrote on June 12, 1971, "Sizable segments of the evangelical movement long have been afflicted with anti-Semitism; Graham's efforts to eradicate this illness have brought him much deserved praise from the nation's Jewish community." [23]

The Evangelist and the Student Movement

During the late 1960's the student movement claimed an increasing amount of Graham's time and attention. On several occasions he would don dark glasses and casual clothes to mingle with young people on campuses such as the strife-torn Morningside Heights area of Columbia University. As early as June 1969 Graham could report that he had held two long meetings with SDS leaders in "trying to understand them." [24]

Graham feared that the student rebellions might result in a wave of reaction which could lead to "demands for suppression of certain liberties." [25] Speaking to students at Anderson-Montreat College on December 13, 1970, he warned that "in our search for new freedom, we are in danger of losing what little freedom we have left." [26] Yet Graham evidenced a grudging respect for the dedication of the youthful rebels. Speaking to a New York crusade audience he quoted from a letter written by a student radical to his girl friend in which the young man said he was ready to go before a firing squad for his ideals. "This sounds like the writings of the early church. Somewhere along the line we've lost the meaning of discipleship." [27]

By the beginning of the decade of the 1970's some observers were wondering whether Graham had lost touch with youth. When the Jesus revolution came into national prominence Graham praised the movement, seeing a net gain for the cause of Christianity despite the anti-Establishment stance of most of the young "Jesus freaks." Later he took a more cautious position and wondered why the Jesus people who seemed to be absorbed in study and communal living were not actively entering into the day-to-day struggle to evangelize the world.

The new decade also brought questions concerning the nature of his constituency and their zeal for Christ. Roy Larson analyzed the 1971 Chicago Crusade and concluded that Graham's followers were getting old. In addition the evangelist did not seem to be able to attract sizable numbers of people unrelated to his "core constituency in Chicago-area evangelical churches" to the McCormick Place meetings. Larson was struck by the lack of drama and originality at the crusade sessions. "The rallies move along as predictably as an Episcopal service based on the Book of Common Prayer. Even when it comes time for the altar call at the end, Graham patiently describes every single thing that will happen when the candidate comes forward for conversion." [28] Larson also deplored what he felt was a tendency to "bland out" and depoliticize some segments of the body politic. "Political slogans are depoliticized—'moral ecology,' 'real peace through God,' 'join the Jesus revolution.' "

Perhaps the most incisive question Larsen raised came at the conclusion of his article: "Is Graham converting people to mainline Biblical Christianity or to mainstream Americanism?" [29] We would add two observations to Larson's analysis: First, what might have been true of the Chicago Crusade would not necessarily be true of other crusades. Thus, there was a large youth contingent present two months later in Oakland, Calif., at the Northern California Crusade. Second, we would contend that in a sociological sense there may be little significant difference between mainline Biblical Christianity and mainline America.

The Evangelist at the Center of American Life

Billy Graham today stands in the closest proximity to the Presidency, to the majority of the nation's Protestants, and to the great center of America's social and political life. Out of the impatience with established order and authority, with church and government, and in the midst of a society wracked by war and internal violence he has emerged as the standard bearer of the new heartland, a region more attitudinal than geographic, the region already being defined by the sociologists as Middle America, the seat of traditional American concepts of morality and action. Our task now is to turn to a description and analysis of Graham's social thought. This will be facilitated by a detailed account of his activities in two crucial areas of contemporary American life: race and politics. Finally we shall attempt to describe the implications his current position suggests for the 1970's with particular emphasis on the 1972 Presidential election.

GRAHAM'S SOCIAL THEORY

It cannot be stressed too strongly that Graham's social thought is grounded in his theological presuppositions. While articulated with growing sophistication, these presuppositions remain true to his early training and educational experiences. Graham's essential beliefs are thoroughly in line with the theological principles which have been the basis of fundamentalism in the twentieth century.[30] On the Charlotte farm and as a student at Bob Jones College, Florida Bible Institute and Wheaton College Graham might be exposed to varying nuances of interpretation and differing moral and spiritual emphases, but neither at home nor in the classroom would he hear any teacher depart from belief in the inspiration and authority of the Bible, the Virgin Birth, the substitutionary death of Christ, the bodily resurrection of Jesus and his second coming.

Doctrinal Foundations

Understanding his particular calling to be that of the evangelist, Graham puts special stress on the need of men to recognize their sinfulness and accept Jesus as personal Lord and Saviour. It is his gift to bring men to the point where in total submission to God they recognize their utter dependence upon Christ's work of redemption at the cross and allow Jesus to come into their lives, to bring salvation. To Graham sin is "missing the target at which life must aim and which life ought to hit." It is a "failure to live up to God's standards." [31] Sin, to be sure, according to the fundamentalist principles of faith, is inherited through Adam's fall; but we are "also sinners by choice." [32] Not only does sin keep man from God, it also has deleterious effects upon his life, personality and human contacts. Sin affects the mind, will and conscience, "so much so that the totality of life is infected . . . darkening his intellect, enfeebling his will, corrupting his emotions." [33] Man is thus "alienated from God and in need of restoration." But sin does more than this, it causes a threefold death: physical, spiritual and eternal.

Only a radical and revolutionary recovery can change this bleak picture. This recovery comes in the form of redemption by God. As Graham says, "Only God can properly diagnose man's disease; only God can provide the remedy." [34] This remedy is the blood of his son, Jesus Christ. Referring to Heb. 9:22 ("Without the shedding of blood there is no forgiveness of sins"), Graham writes, "When Jesus Christ, the perfect God-man, shed his blood on the cross, He was surrendering His pure and spotless life to death as an eternal sacrifice for man's sin. Once for all God made complete and perfect provision for the cure for man's sins; without the blood of Christ, it is indeed a fatal disease." [35] If man will believe this he will be saved and he will become a new person. Graham repeatedly refers to the verse in Romans, "If any man be in Christ he is a new person, old things are put away, all things are become new." [36] This new birth is more than a reformation, it is a transformation. A new life has been born in the person's soul. He receives a new nature and a new heart. He becomes a new creation. It is crucial to understand this delineation of the new birth if one is to come to grips with Graham's social thought. The new birth changes a man so radically that where there was once intolerance, prejudice, ill will, there is now love, fellowship and new brotherhood.

Answering the claim that the problems of race and war will never be solved, Graham points to the new birth:

> I say that these and all other problems can be solved, but only at the Cross. The cross of Christ is not only the basis of our peace and hope; but it is also the means of our eternal salvation. The object of the cross is not only a full and free pardon; it is also a changed life, lived in fellowship with God. This is the message for the world today. This is the message of hope and peace and brotherhood.[37]

The concepts of sin and redemption and the new birth in Graham's theological system share paramount importance with the second coming of Christ. Man the sinner, redeemed by the blood of Jesus, transformed into a new creation, manifesting godly traits in his earthly experiences anxiously awaits the return of Christ, an event which will signal the end of the world as it is now known and the beginning of a new and eternal age of peace and joy. The second coming will be an absolute and totally revolutionary experience. It will "change every aspect of life on this planet. Christ will reign in righteousness. Disease will be arrested. Death will be modified. War will be abolished. Nature will be changed. Man will live as it was originally intended he should live." [38] According to Graham there are many signs of the imminence of Christ's return: war, violence, lawlessness, personal and group immorality, a falling away from genuine Christian faith, persecution of those Christians who retain allegiance to Christ, and an increase in mass evangelism to worldwide proportions.[39] Knowledge of the second coming, says Graham, should cause Christians to "evangelize with zeal, intensify worldwide mission efforts, intensify social concern, guard against theological error, live holy lives and give hope and comfort to other people." [40]

Graham's belief in individual salvation makes him skeptical of all plans and programs which claim to bring about corporate amelioration of evil. Influenced by neo-evangelicalism, he would concede the importance of social concern and humanitarian activities on the part of Christians, but he would not agree that such interest and efforts are a complete fulfillment of Christian responsibility to the well-being of the whole fellow man. Thus Carl F. H. Henry, who suggests that the only meaningful manifestations of social reform which have occurred in the last hundred years resulted from the actions of evangelicals also insists that the ultimate act of humanitarianism is the witness to salvation in Christ given by a Christian to a non-Christian.[41] In confronting every social problem, the evangelical sees personal salvation as the key which will bring amelioration. Society will be changed for the better only when individuals accept Christ as saviour. For when this happens they become new people and begin to take on the fruits of the spirit: love, joy, patience, righteousness, justice, peace.[42]

This differs sharply from the view of the nonevangelical Christian who comes to each social problem asking, What would Jesus do in this situation? The approach might be socialistic (dividing the loaves and fishes) or punitive (driving the money changers from the temple) or passive (rendering to Caesar what is his). Identification with Jesus is important to both evangelical and liberal Christian, but their modes of identification are vastly different. To the evangelical, Jesus is the suffering servant of Isaiah 53 who has given his life as an offering for personal sin. The evangelical thus identifies with Jesus in his suffering (Galatians 2:20) [43] and with those sayings which suggest that trouble and persecution will be the Christian's portion as he walks as a stranger and pilgrim through an ungodly world. On this pilgrimage he may give a cup of water to a little one, visit the sick, even sell all that he has and give the proceeds to the poor; but above all he must lose no opportunity to witness to the saving power of Jesus, to the personal redemption offered at Calvary. The liberal identifies with what appears to have been the focus of Jesus' ministry prior to the cross: to preach the gospel to the poor, to bring release to the prisoner, to set at liberty the captive. Hence, while to many evangelicals the Sermon on the Mount has only eschatological meaning, to liberals it is a blueprint for healing the wounds of contemporary society.

The Evangelical vs. The Liberal View of the Church

The difference in outlook between eschatological hope and present achievement points up the difference in evangelical and liberal views of the role of the church in society. To evangelicals the church is a called-out body of believers, the vehicle through which the message of individual salvation is communicated to a lost world. To the liberal, the church is the broker through which Christ reconciles man to man and all to himself. While distressed by societal problems, the evangelical expects only a continuation and intensification of human strife until the second coming of Jesus. Works of charity should be carried out to aid in immediate, local problems, but the main thrust of Christian activity should be toward bringing as many souls as possible into the church before the return of Jesus. The very problems which increasingly occupy so much of the time and resources of the liberal community point to the fact that the end of the age is at hand, that the final, cataclysmic events of history are about to unfold.

This sense of urgency is also present in liberal thought, but leads to different theory and action. As crises deepen, the threat of catastrophe indeed seems to hang over the human family. Time seems to be running out and in such a situation desperate risks must be taken. Dr. Archie Hargraves, former director of the Chicago-based Urban Training Institute, suggested several years ago that the church must "move into the action" even if not certain as to all of the issues and nuances involved in a particular situation.[44] To more radical thinkers the church as the institution we now know must pass away; like Jesus it must die for the sins of men and redeem the greater society. This apocalyptic view of the demise of organized Christianity would differ sharply from Graham's understanding of the role of the church as a witnessing agent in a sin-riddled world. To be sure, the church as an institution will one day see its mission fulfilled, but that will occur at an hour which no one can predict, at the return of Jesus to earth. Until then Graham and his associates will continue to conduct their ministry within the organized body of Christ.

For some fundamentalists the tension between living in a sin-pervaded world and awaiting the return of Christ is too great and they move to one of two extremes. Some stress personal pietism while others become overly occupied with the political configurations of the society in which they live.[45] Graham's reply to a recent question asking how he balances his belief in the second coming with an active interest in the social and political life of the nation indicates that he has successfully maintained a balance between the two worlds.

> The second coming must be viewed first of all as an historical event yet to take place. It is also the nature of a hope that has been given to Christians and in anticipation of this hope God has given great encouragement to his church particularly in times of extreme suffering and need. The second coming, therefore, has a timeless quality about it and it is with this in mind that I can feel so free in proclaiming the second coming of Christ as being a glorious hope given to the church without the necessity of establishing a date. Having said this, it is of the very nature of Christian concern that we become aware of social needs and wherever possible we do all that can be done

to alleviate the suffering of humanity. This is a matter of Christian principle. And also the Christian is a citizen of two worlds. He is a citizen of this world in which he is now living, and living here he has certain responsibility. . . . Therefore in becoming politically involved and having a tremendous interest in our nation's well-being I cannot help but feel that this is rendering to Caesar the things that are Caesar's. I have this as a Christian responsibility as does every Christian . . . to become very much involved in the alleviation of the suffering of humanity through personal involvement and also retaining that blessed hope of the glorious appearing of our great God and Saviour Jesus Christ.[46]

Writing in *Christianity Today* Graham returned to this theme:

> We as Christians have two responsibilities: first to proclaim the Gospel of Jesus Christ as the only answer to man's deepest needs; and second, to apply as best we can the principles of Christianity to the social conditions around us.[47]

The Limits of Social Involvement

This philosophy has been foreign, especially in recent years, to activists in the World and National Councils of Churches and in the major denominations. Speaking at the World Congress on Evangelism in 1964 Graham criticized some ministers who substituted "the race question for the Gospel, making it their gospel." [48] In a similar vein he has attacked church leaders who "have become angry with the world and are determined to use violence to change the social structures of society." [49] To Graham the overly social-action-minded clergy misread the mind and mood of their constituents. Commenting on the 1968 U.S. Conference on Church and Society held in Detroit the evangelist said:

> Thousands of laymen and clergymen alike are asking penetrating questions about the purpose and mission of the church . . . many of them are becoming disillusioned with the institutional church; they are hungry for a personal vital experience with Jesus Christ.[50]

Graham's claim has, of course, been widely disputed by many churchmen. Thus at a meeting of the General Assembly of the National Council of Churches, the Council's secretary for Christian Life and Mission, the Rev. Colin W. Williams, charged Graham with emphasizing the personal nature of conversion to such an extent that he lost sight of the social dimensions of human evil. Such evangelism, Williams concluded, "is no longer an adequate symbol for the contemporary world." [51] Graham at the same meeting issued a sharp criticism of churchmen who "call for social service without also providing a solid spiritual basis for it." [52]

The activist position notwithstanding, the fact is that for the last several years the mainline Protestant denominations have experienced loss of income and grass-roots support. Membership has fallen off in most major communions and program and personnel cuts have been made. That the recession cannot entirely be blamed for this is evidenced by the membership growth of evangelical groups such as the Assemblies of God, the Evangelical Free Church, and the Southern Baptist Convention. The great hue and cry which arose in the ranks of the United Presbyterian Church when that body's General Assembly authorized a ten-thousand dollar grant to the Angela Davis defense fund graphically illustrates how far apart church leadership and their constituencies are in the area of social reform. At this point in American church history the activists are increasingly being isolated as Graham and those who feel the pendulum has swung too far away from the redemptive witness of the gospel gain an ever-widening circle of adherents.

The Evangelicals and Social Reform

It should also be noted that Graham has the capacity for self-criticism on social issues. Speaking to the 1971 meeting of the National Association of Evangelicals, he urged his listeners to maintain interest in social activity.

> Many of the great social movements of this generation were founded by evangelicals but for about a generation we allowed liberals and radicals to take the ball from us.[53]

A similar view was expressed by theologian Carl F. H. Henry at Eastern Mennonite College in February 1971. After stating that "fundamentalism has too long identified itself with the status quo," Henry called upon evangelicals to face up to the problems posed by the modern world:

> Evangelical Christianity faces the choice of either retreating to the Dead Sea caves, or taking an initiative that places modern man on the defensive amid his moral and spiritual compromise.[54]

It may well be, given the context of contemporary American church and political life, that Graham and the evangelicals can make a greater contribution to needed social reform than can the radicals and activists. We need only recall the contributions to social reform made by evangelical Protestants in England during the early part of the nineteenth century. Leaders such as Henry Thornton of Elapham, William Wilberforce, and John Newton agitated for the abolition of the slave trade as well as for industrial and prison reform. Examples of the involvement of revivalism in American social reform include the following: George Whitefield (originally an associate of the Wesleys) collected funds for orphans, free blacks, and German Reformed and Mennonite immigrants during his successful open-air revival meetings; of the nine colonial colleges, the six established between 1740 and 1769 were related directly or indirectly to the revivals of the period; under the rule of president Charles Grandison Finney, the outstanding evangelist of the mid-nineteenth century, Ohio's Oberlin College served not only as a model for educational innovation (e.g. coeducation) but as a center of abolitionist activity.

There is a more sharply focused realism to Graham's position because he understands the limits within which he and the religious bodies may act without seriously undermining their very existence as authentic representatives of faith perspectives held by the majority of Christians. The reaction by activists within the major denominations as well as by a significant number of National Council of Churches staff to James Forman's call for reparations, indicates the lengths to which some churchmen are prepared to go in order to actualize their vision of a just society. These individuals believe that Christian love and the goal of bringing righteousness and justice to a sick and racist America call for a positive reaction to every demand of those who have been wronged, especially when these wrongs have resulted at least in part from the actions of Christians. Thus every demand no matter how unreasonable, potentially destructive or representative of a non-Christian ideology (Marx, Che, Mao) must be met with an acknowledgment of guilt accompanied by acquiescence to at least part of the request. The authors well remember a visit to the Interchurch Center in New York during the period Forman and his associates were occupying various offices of the National Council and several denominations. On one floor, which had not as yet been visited by Forman, several staff members had brought sleeping bags from home anxiously awaiting the moment of "liberation." [55] Such attempts to act out fantasies of how the church and larger society can honestly and effectively confront the deep and continuing social crisis indicate the distance some have traveled from a traditional understanding of the interaction of church and society. In his call for responsible Christian citizenship, based on the concept of corporate change through individual salvation, Graham remains closer to the mental and emotional bent of most Americans who seriously desire meaningful social reform, without sacrificing his credibility as a representative of the historic Christian faith.

GRAHAM AND RACE

The evangelist's early life was spent in a society which championed segregation. There is little evidence that prior to his matriculation at Wheaton College Graham differed from other young men of his age and background in terms of his understanding of the worth, place and role of Negroes. At Wheaton, Graham majored in anthropology and found the Biblical and scientific "proofs" of Negro inferiority unconvincing. Yet it was not until 1953 that he insisted upon the integration of his crusade audiences. The seating of Negroes with whites at Chattanooga in March of that year ended the prevailing Southern norm of segregated seating that had existed at crusades in twelve Southern cities since the Charlotte meeting in November of 1947.

It should also be pointed out that neither at Wheaton nor in Youth for Christ and early crusade settings did Graham come into contact with any significant number of theologically like-minded Negroes. Indeed evangelical Protestantism in the 1940's and '50's was overwhelmingly white, and conservative on the question of race. As late as 1960 Wheaton's sister school, Gordon College of Massachusetts, could count but five Negro students out of a total of four hundred, while at about the same time the famed Moody Bible Institute had only ten registered Negroes in its student body—seven of whom came from African countries. During the period of Graham's rise to leadership within evangelicalism, few pastors had pulpit or personal fellowship with their Negro counterparts. Although evangelicals stressed the revolutionary nature of the gospel, especially in its capacity to break down barriers which divided brothers in Christ, they went along with the prevailing attitudes on race in both the North and the South. When the Moody Chorale toured Virginia in 1958 the three Negro members of the group remained in Chicago. The desire to conform to local fashion concerning mixed dating was so intense at Moody that a young man was ordered to refrain from escorting a dark skinned Puerto Rican girl student to the downtown area, lest the school's "witness" be compromised. Neither Moody nor any other major or, for that matter, minor evangelical school had a Negro faculty member or trustee until well into the 1960's.

The Rejection of Segregation

By that time Graham had moved far ahead of his contemporaries in evangelicalism, boasting as early as 1960 that "we've held integrated crusades in every Southern state save Georgia, Alabama and Mississippi and have not had a single incident." [56] In the same year he criticized segregation within the church:

> How does one explain why, of all of America's great institutions, the Christian Church is still the most segregated? It has become a byword that 'the most segregated hour of the week is still eleven o'clock Sunday morning.' This is true of churches in the North as well as in the South.[57]

By the early sixties Graham had integrated his team with the addition of Howard Jones of Cleveland. Later he would bring to his staff Ralph Bell, a gifted young Negro graduate of Taylor University. When the sit-ins and demonstrations developed into a full-fledged movement with national implications at the beginning of the sixties Graham began to react publicly to the racial crisis. On May 17, 1961 after Freedom Riders had been attacked in Anniston and Montgomery, Ala., Graham urged that the culprits be prosecuted to "the full extent of the law." Speaking at a news conference aboard the *Queen Elizabeth* as he was about to leave for a crusade in Manchester, England, he added "I think it is deplorable when certain people in any society have been treated as second-class citizens." [58]

Two years later, however, the Birmingham, Ala., sit-ins and marches led by Martin Luther King came under criticism from Graham. On May 18, 1963, after several hundred people had been arrested, Graham suggested that King "put the brakes on a little bit." He called for "a period of quietness in which moderation prevails." [59] Graham also voiced serious doubt that the Birmingham Negro community supported the demonstrations. This brought an angry objection from the Fellowship of Reconciliation, a religious pacifist organization. On April 25 the Fellowship's National Council issued a statement which called Graham's suggestion to curtail the demonstrations, "a grievous error." [60]

Birmingham in 1964: An Integrated Audience

In September Graham stated that he would hold an integrated crusade in Birmingham if clergymen of both races would invite him. A crusade did not materialize, but on Easter Sunday of 1964 Graham made history by preaching to an integrated audience of 50,000 in Birmingham's Legion Field.[61] Invited by a biracial committee of Protestant, Roman Catholic and Jewish laymen as a response to the September 1963 bombing of the Sixteenth Street Baptist Church in which four Negro girls were killed, Graham called for a new effort by all men to end prejudice in America. Although his message stressed national issues, the significance for Birmingham was clear. Graham sensed this when, standing on the platform below the Negro section of the city known as "Dynamite Hill," he said, "What a moment and what an hour for Birmingham. It is good to stand together for Christ." [62] At the conclusion of the service the Rev. J. L. Ware, a local Negro clergyman, commented that the session may have signaled the beginning of a new period of racial peace in the troubled Alabama city.[63]

It is important to note that Graham described the racial crisis within the larger context of human depravity. "We are now beginning to realize that something is desperately wrong with human nature. The most burning question of our times is the problem of man. What causes the hate, prejudice, lust, immorality, greed, deceit, fraud and war that we read and hear about each day?" [64] The fact that Graham was invited by laymen indicated the continuing lack of communication between the city's Negro and white clergy. This situation was pointedly brought home to one of the authors at the September funeral of three of the girls killed in the blast at the Sixteenth Street Baptist Church. As clergy waited under the trees of a nearby Catholic church to begin a walk to the service, a group of white and black Methodist ministers stood in a circle with almost no conversation occurring—this despite the presence of Bishop Charles Golden of the then segregated Central Jurisdiction of The Methodist Church.

Speaking to newsmen in Chicago in April, Graham pointed to the Easter service in Birmingham as an example of the efficacy of interracial mass rallies. This, rather than "demonstrations in the streets and the civil rights bill," would help to solve the nation's racial crisis. In Birmingham, Graham said, "over 4,000 came forward at the close [to make a decision for Christ] and I would say that much of the prejudice was leaving in the spiritual context. We must preach the Gospel of Christ, not race, such efforts can be of immense help in this racial misunderstanding." [65] The next day Graham said much the same thing to an audience more important to his ministry than a group of newsmen. Appearing before the annual meeting of the National Association of Evangelicals on April 7, he asked evangelical leaders to assume greater responsibility in solving the racial crisis. Addressing a body not normally given to self-criticism Graham noted that some Christian colleges and Bible schools had been slow to desegregate. He declared,

> We should have been leading the way to racial justice but we failed, let's confess it, let's admit it and let's do something about it.[66]

In May, speaking at the University of North Carolina, Graham made what was considered his strongest statement to date on race: "Those people who say they can prove segregation from the Bible don't know their Bible." [67] The real message of the Bible, he told 16,000 persons in Kenan Stadium, is "love thy neighbor as thyself."

By June of 1693, Graham was predicting a long, hot, bloody summer as America faced an internal crisis as great as that faced by Abraham Lincoln at the beginning of the Civil War. This crisis could only be resolved "when the hearts of men and women have been transformed and made to love instead of hate." [68] Graham issued a prescient warning to the thousands of white suburbanites gathered at Arlington Park Race Track. "America has to get back to God in the next five or six years or we will face troubles and bloodshed such as you cannot dream about in your suburban homes." [69] By the fall of 1964 Graham was convinced that the South was nearer than the North to solving its racial problems. "The South has few ghettos and is making rapid progress toward integration." [70]

Focusing on Rights

In early March of 1965 Graham told a group of students who met with him in Honolulu that perhaps he personally had not done enough on the race question. Replying to a question which implied inaction on his part, Graham said, "It's true I haven't been in jail yet. I underscore the word *yet*. Maybe I haven't done all I could or should do." [71] In the same meeting, however, Graham noted that he had recently received the George Washington Carver Award for his contributions to race relations. Several days later on March 13 Graham urged President Lyndon Johnson to meet face to face with leaders of both sides in the deepening Alabama civil rights crisis.[72] On April 11 he announced cancellation of engagements in Great Britain in order to comply with urgent requests made by white and Negro clergymen that he hold meetings in Alabama.[73] This act gained him national attention and a few days later the New York *Times* carried a long article under the head, "BILLY GRAHAM IS FOCUSING ON RIGHTS." [74] In a wide-ranging interview with reporter Paul Montgomery, Graham rejected claims that the Bible supports segregation and bars intermarriage. He also spoke in favor of the Civil Rights Act of 1964 and the pending voting rights legislation. As far as demonstrations were concerned, "I never felt that we should attain our rights by illegal means, yet I must confess that the demonstrations have served to arouse the conscience of the world." [75]

Late in April Graham moved into Alabama, holding meetings in Dothan, and at the University of Alabama, Auburn University, and Tuskegee Institute. In Dothan the meetings conducted by Graham and members of his staff were the first interracial gatherings in the city's history. Commenting on the sessions, the Rev. Clayton Bell, minister of the First Presbyterian Church, stressed a theme common to racial moderates:

> Not only was there no conflict . . . but a genuine spirit of love and fellowship which was totally devoid of pretension captivated the hearts of those present. I feel a deep sense of satisfaction in having been vindicated in a contention that I have made, along with many other ministers in our South, that when the gospel of Jesus Christ is applied to the hearts of people, problems which otherwise loom too large become small and even disappear.[76]

Among the important by-products of Graham's visit were the biracial meetings of local leaders who came together to confer with the evangelist. Religious News Service reported that at one such meeting—the first in which Negro and white leaders had dined together—a Baptist layman was quoted by a Graham aide as saying that though he had long been prejudiced against the Negro, he was now convinced that "if we are to win the world for Christ, we're going to have to be color blind." [77]

In his public comments Graham seemed to be carving out a middle-ground position. On April 25, speaking on the Hour of Decision (heard in Alabama), he said that Alabama's story had been distorted by the "world's newspapers." There was no state where more people went to church on Sunday morning, and "friendship between the whites and the Negroes in Alabama is very deep." Further the state could solve its racial problems if "extremists both to the left and to the right can be controlled." [78] The Alabama tour was climaxed two months later with a hastily arranged eight-day crusade in Montgomery, capital of the state and cradle of the Confederacy. While in town Graham took the opportunity to visit with Governor George Wallace. Though declining to reveal details of their conversation Graham admitted that "we did discuss social issues." [79] For his part Wallace issued a statement through his press secretary in which he expressed pleasure at the Graham visit. Repeating the earlier Alabama experience Graham also met with pastors and lay people as well as with several hundred members of the city's civic clubs. By the end of the crusade Graham had spoken to 100,000 residents in the first major biracial event in the capital's history. On June 21 Graham stated that the Montgomery experience was "the most rewarding and thrilling of my ministry. Night after night I watched hundreds of people of both races march not with hatred but in unity and a spirit of love as Christ drew them together." [80] Summing up the impact of the meetings Graham saw the creation of new atmosphere, "a change in the spiritual and social climate of major proportions." Progress could continue "if the Ku Klux Klan will give Alabama time to digest the new civil rights laws, and if the politicians will not try to exploit the situation." [81]

Riot in Watts

Two months later the attention of the nation focused on the bloody site of a new racial battleground, the section of south central Los Angeles known as Watts. At home in Montreat as the riots broke out, Graham quickly made plans to fly to Los Angeles. On the night before he left he told a crowd at the Presbyterian retreat grounds that the Los Angeles riot was only "a dress rehearsal of what is to come." [82] One answer to head off a possible blood bath would be for Congress to "immediately drop all other legislation and devise new laws to deal with riots and violence. . . . We need drastic laws to deal with subversives of the right and left that are preaching hate." Yet in the final analysis even laws will not solve the racial crisis. Returning to a theme he has consistently articulated throughout his ministry, Graham told the overflow crowd:

> Laws and legislation are not enough. We must have a spiritual awakening that changes the human heart. Hate, resentment and prejudices come from within and cannot be legislated out of man.[83]

Upon arrival in Los Angeles Graham received a "first-class, red-carpet briefing" from state, city and National Guard officials led by Governor Brown.[84] He then donned a bulletproof vest and viewed the riot area from the bulletproof seat of a police helicopter. He concluded that the great majority of residents had nothing to do with the trouble, but that extremists played a major role in leading the disturbance. Graham correctly analyzed the mood and shock of the nation at the Watts situation when he told reporters in Denver on August 26, "I believe the riots have hurt the civil rights cause. People across the nation are afraid, baffled and bewildered by what happened in Los Angeles." [85] Throughout the remainder of the 1960's Graham continued to stress this theme. At a news conference in Montreat he asked why governmental authorities had failed to see that riots could not have been executed without prior planning and organization.[86] By July of the next year Graham was appealing to President Johnson to identify the groups inside America "who are teaching and advocating violence, training in guerrilla tactics and defying authority." [87] Speaking on the Hour of Decision a month later Graham stated:

> The majority of the American people want law, order and security in our society. There is no doubt that the rioting, looting and crime in America this summer has reached the point of anarchy.[88]

Graham rejected claims that poverty was a major contributing factor to the riots which that summer had brought devastation to wide areas of Newark and Detroit.

> We have been told over and over again by some of our leaders in Washington that poverty is the cause of crime. This just is not true. There was no such rioting, looting, or killing

of police officers in depression days when people were much poorer.[89]

As in the past Graham's remedy was a proper relationship to Christ, although he maintained that "tough laws against the subversive elements that are openly seeking the overthrow of the government" would also help.

As the riots ended and the Black Power movement faded, Graham, like most Americans, turned his attention to the 1968 Presidential campaign, Vietnam, and issues such as church-state relations and pornography. Then in 1969, during his Anaheim, Calif., crusade, he met with one of the country's major black evangelicals, Dr. Edward V. Hill, pastor of Mount Zion Baptist Church in Watts and president of the Los Angeles Fire Commission. The session, held at Graham's request, was scheduled to last forty minutes but Hill remained for six hours "laying it on the line," as he recalled it in an interview with the authors.[90] Hill, whose ministry evidenced remarkable results in both the spiritual and secular realms, told Graham of the unrest among Negro evangelicals and of their impatience with white Christian brothers who seemed to have little interest in their problems. As a result of the meeting Graham and Hill brought together the country's leading black evangelicals in October. Graham, who addressed the Kansas City session, spent most of the time sitting in the audience using the sessions as a learning experience. Out of the contact with Hill came mutual respect and a continuing association. It was Hill who acted as master of ceremonies at the "Honor America Day" religious service and it was from the pulpit of Hill's church that Graham announced plans for a crusade to be held in Watts in 1972. Hill, whose church operates a credit union, builds senior citizens' housing and conducts a Christian training institute, has recently appeared at Graham crusades in Chicago and Oakland. In 1970 he joined eleven other black churchmen at a meeting in the White House convened by Graham and attended by President Nixon.[91]

Ahead of His Constituency

In a recent interview Graham was asked whether his personal interest in bringing white and black evangelicals together will have significant grass-roots effect. The evangelist responded by pointing to the co-operation between blacks and whites which has marked his crusades since the early fifties. He then said "I do not feel however this has extended very far . . . beyond our crusades. I would be very reluctant to say that it has strengthened relationships on and across the board at grass-roots level." [92] This characteristically honest answer would be seconded by younger black evangelicals such as evangelist Tom Skinner and Rev. Michael Haynes, pastor of Boston's Twelfth Street Baptist Church. Skinner, who has appeared at several national evangelical meetings over the past few years, has been an outspoken critic of his white brethren. In a recent interview conducted at the 1971 Jerusalem Conference on Biblical Prophecy, Skinner and Haynes, who also serves as Commissioner of Parole for the Commonwealth of Massachusetts, described the tokenism which is characteristic of current evangelicalism. Both felt Graham could do more but were somewhat vague as to specifics.[93]

Graham, who has consistently been far ahead of his constituency on race, is thus cast in the role of mediator between the younger militant black evangelical and the older white evangelical leadership which still feels uncomfortable worshipping and fellowshipping with black brothers. Clearly Graham has moved beyond the white evangelical leadership in his alliance with men such as E. V. Hill, yet he is attacked by blacks in the denominations who accuse him of continuing relationships with racist elements in the church. Recently J. Metz Rollins, Jr., executive secretary of the National Committee of Black Churchmen and a Presbyterian minister, called Graham one of the most dangerous forces in the country. Speaking in Atlanta on November 22, 1970, Rollins said Graham "preaches an individualistic type gospel which puts country above people and justice." [94]

It may be that Rollins, like Skinner and Haynes, expects too much of Graham and has a distorted understanding of just what Graham can do. If one objectively examines Graham's actions and statements over the last ten years it would be difficult to conclude that he has been silent or even cautious on race.[95] When one considers his background, constituency, and the mood of the nation as a whole, he has come very far and can be expected to go further. It must also be stated that Graham is subject to definite limitations—he holds no political office or ecclesiastical post within the mainline or fundamentalist churches. His vast influence is based on his ministry as the most successful evangelist of his age. Finally, Graham's basic theological commitment will always keep him from an extreme position concerning the amelioration of real or imagined wrongs. In evaluating Graham's actions one must never forget that he firmly believes that ultimate change can come only within the context of a society, all of whose members are personally redeemed. Similarly the Apostle Paul who lived in a society which contenanced slavery did not directly condemn the practice but "his message that every man is of immeasurable value in the sight of God helped eventually to free the slaves." [96] Writing in *The Presbyterian Journal* Graham succinctly articulated his position when he said:

> The only way to change men is to get them converted to Jesus Christ. Then they will have the capacity to live up to the Christian command: "Love thy neighbor." [96]

GRAHAM AND POLITICS

From the beginning of his ministry Graham evidenced keen interest in the political life of the nation. As early as 1948 a governor appeared on one of his crusade platforms and by 1950 he had his first meeting with an incumbent

President. Graham's call in the early fifties for a crusade to change the spiritual and moral tone of America gave theological breadth to the basic theme of the Eisenhower Administration. While not a close personal friend of the general, Graham nonetheless had several meetings with Eisenhower and the two men shared a genuine mutual respect. When it became apparent well before the 1960 Presidential campaign began that the Democratic party might nominate a Roman Catholic, immense pressures were put on Graham not only to support the Republican nominee who would probably be his friend Richard Nixon but to reject publicly the very idea of a Catholic Presidential candidate.

By early summer of 1960 petitions were circulating in evangelical congregations throughout the country calling upon the major parties to refrain from nominating a Roman Catholic for the nation's highest office. The authors (both of whom were Congregational pastors at the time) well remember the consternation of several congregants when they refused to sign such petitions after June worship services. The campaign also engendered vocal and often vicious anti-Catholic propaganda from the offices of Bob Jones, Carl McIntire, and the late cowboy evangelist of the Rockies, Harvey Springer, who boasted that he had a secret weapon which would defeat Kennedy on Election Day.[97] Even the more respected evangelical leadership fell victim to the emotionalism sparked by the prospect of a Roman Catholic in the White House. Warnings of sinister things to come if Kennedy were elected came from the headquarters of the National Association of Evangelicals[98] and *Christianity Today*.[99]

On evangelical college campuses Nixon was an overwhelming favorite and any students who sported Kennedy buttons were liable to have their spiritual as well as political judgment called into question. At Graham's alma mater, Wheaton College, the administration allowed free use of the college mail service to Nixon supporters but required the few Kennedy adherents to mail their literature through regular paid channels. Several weeks before the election, a group of evangelical leaders, joined by Norman Vincent Peale, met in Washington and questioned whether a Roman Catholic President could be free of ties to the Vatican.[100] Graham, who was scheduled to appear at the meeting, did not attend; consequently, as Edward Fiske, religion editor of the New York *Times,* points out, he did not suffer Peale's resultant loss of prestige when the Massachusetts Senator entered the White House.[101]

Kennedy, realizing that the mounting opposition from conservative Protestants could swing the election to Nixon, went into the lion's den and met with a large group of Houston ministers. This session, arranged by staff member Jim Wine, a former official of the National Council of Churches, enabled Kennedy to quell the wild speculation as to what he would do if elected, and gave concrete answers as to how he intended to relate to the Roman hierarchy. Graham resisted all pressure to endorse Nixon, but on November 3, just five days before the election, he flew to Columbia, S.C., to give the invocation at a Nixon rally. Just prior to the rally Nixon and Graham appeared on the steps of the state house together and then, as the band played "Dixie is No Longer in the Bag," the two men strode down the steps under a banner emblazoned with the same motto. This act was widely reported in the press and to some observers seemed to have the effect of an endorsement. Mr. Nixon had apparently learned some lessons from Kennedy's successful wooing of conservative Protestants. In the years that followed he would find many ways to call attention to his close friendship with America's best known evangelical leader.

Relations with Two Democratic Presidents

The restrained favoritism which Graham showed toward his friend Richard Nixon did not prevent President-elect Kennedy from establishing public ties with the evangelist. On January 16, 1961, Graham, who was conducting a crusade in Jacksonville, traveled to Palm Beach to confer, lunch and play a round of golf with the President-elect.[102] The meeting, arranged by a mutual friend, Senator George Smathers, took the press and nation by surprise. At a press conference that night in the Towers Hotel, Kennedy and Graham stood side by side and exchanged compliments.

Graham told the press that JFK's election had helped relations between Protestant and Catholic churches. He added, "I think also that his election proved that there was not as much religious prejudice in the United States as many people feared." [103] He praised Kennedy for facing the religious issue "forthrightly" thereby easing many fears held by some voters about a Catholic in the White House.[104] In answer to a question concerning the November 3 Columbia rally Graham stated, "I did not commit myself on the religious issue before the election. I made no statement whatsoever before the election on the matter of religion." [105] During the Kennedy years Graham visited with the President several times, but was in no way an intimate friend or advisor. He backed Kennedy's policy during the Cuban missile crisis of 1962,[106] and in the same year took a firm position in favor of a referendum on Bible reading in the public schools.[107] There was some speculation that Kennedy sought Graham as an ally when he attempted to make good his pledge on strict separation of church and state against mounting pressure from the hierarchy and some sections of Protestantism.[108]

In 1963 Graham took issue with one of the pet programs of the New Frontier. Speaking at the Los Angeles Crusade he claimed that the "[Peace] Corps is almost completely materialistic in its aims. Without God at its center it cannot possibly accomplish all that we might hope for it." [109] The Corps director R. Sargent Shriver characterized Graham's remarks as "unfortunate." He added that Graham's claim was without justification and could not be substantiated. Shriver then turned the tables on the evangelist by pointing out that the Corps had been endorsed by Graham's own denomination, the Southern Baptist Convention.[110] He could have added that a key figure in the administration of the program was Billy Don Moyers, a graduate of the Convention's Southwestern Seminary. After the assassination of President Kennedy Graham was invited by then Attorney General Robert F. Kennedy to sit in a special section at St. Matthew's Cathedral reserved for friends of the late President.

The Johnson years saw Graham often at the White House. Graham and Johnson had been acquaintances since the early fifties, and they now became close friends. At times the friendship was strained—particularly when Johnson policies conflicted with the views of Graham and his conservative Protestant constituency. But Graham remained loyal to the Texan and often commented publicly on the difficulties confronting the nation's highest officeholder. On one such occasion Graham recalled how he and his wife visited the President's room at 1 A.M. "Lying on his bed were envelopes filled with documents that the President had to read before he went to bed. In the lonely hours of that room the President had to make decisions that affect the lives of millions around the world." [111] Graham then told his listeners at the 1965 Governors' Prayer Breakfast in Minneapolis that he and Mrs. Graham had resolved to redouble their prayers for the President. He added that all Americans should pray for the President and other public officials and rededicate themselves to "the spiritual principles that made America great." [112]

Graham's relationship with Johnson was severely tried during the 1964 Presidential campaign. His basic theological constituency favored Senator Goldwater. Graham, who throughout the campaign maintained neutrality, received 60,000 telegrams at Montreat, N.C., on November 2 urging him to endorse the Arizonan.[113] As early as the previous summer he had received mail criticizing his association with the President. In September Graham told a news conference that his association with Johnson did not imply politics.[114] He pointed out that he had tried to be friendly with people in both political parties and specifically mentioned his relationship with former Vice President Nixon. This relationship would be subjected to careful scrutiny when the next Presidential campaign opened.

By early 1965 Graham was characterized by some as Chaplain of the White House. Graham laughed off this assertion, but did speak of his great admiration for the President who in "many ways carries the heaviest load of any man since Lincoln." He continued "I think we need unity and should pray for the President that God will help him. I have a sense he is depending on God and looking for his guidance in many directions." Graham concluded that "no one can imagine the loneliness in which the President must make his decisions."[115]

Later in the year Washington columnist Marianne Means wrote perceptively of the relationship between the two men:

> It is understandable that they should get along well. For there is a great deal of preacher in Lyndon Johnson and a great deal of the politician in Billy Graham. Each, in his way, is a dedicated but utterly realistic man. They are both products of the Southern Bible Belt; they share a fervent homespun eloquence which has enabled them to stir the emotions of other men and rise to the peak of their professions.[116]

In November Johnson became the first President to attend a Graham crusade, as he and Lady Bird joined 60,000 constituents to hear Graham preach at the Astrodome.[117]

Graham was also a frequent visitor to the LBJ ranch where he and the President would discuss Vietnam and other crucial issues. In an interview with Edward Fiske, Graham recalled that Johnson often asked for counsel when he faced personal problems. Thus the two men met after the Walter Jenkins scandal broke. Summing up his affection for Johnson, Graham told Fiske:

> I love to be around him because I love Texas and he's all Texas. And I think you have to be in that Pedernales River Valley to understand President Johnson. I understand a little bit of the background of where he came from and what his

roots were and what made him tick. And the things people thought of as crude were not crude to me, because I had been there and I knew that that is the part of Texas he came from.[118]

Johnson for his part favorably described Graham in a letter to the evangelist's official biographer, John Pollock:

> In countries around the world as well as in the United States, he has opened many hearts and doors that were once shuttered. His deep and overwhelming Christian belief is something that cannot be contained by the boundaries of nations or even by difference of religion. People everywhere have come to listen, to love and be influenced by him. He has brought God's Word and His work closer to all of us. Every man is his friend and brother. Anyone who has a close relationship with him as I do, can never forget what it is like to have his companionship and his compassion and to be better because of it. As President there were many times that he sustained and strengthened me through his inspiration and faith, and I am pleased that President Nixon has the comfort and benefit of his prayers and his friendship.[119]

The bridging role Graham played between the two Administrations was nowhere more apparent than when Graham joined Johnson at the White House for his last weekend as President and then offered the major prayer at Nixon's inauguration.

Graham and Richard Nixon

Remarkably enough Graham had met Nixon's parents before he became acquainted with the future President. Preaching at a Youth for Christ rally in Whittier, Calif. in 1948, the evangelist had become acquainted with the Nixons. Graham was particularly impressed by the Nixons' faithful attendance at each nightly session.[120] The Nixons were Quakers but of an evangelical bent, and they, like Frank and Morrow Graham, had the joy of seeing their son make a commitment to Christ in his teen years.[121]

In 1950 Graham and Senator Clyde Hoey of North

Carolina were lunching in the Senate Dining Room when Nixon walked by. Hoey invited Nixon to his table and after several pleasantries were exchanged Nixon asked Graham to join him that afternoon at the Burning Tree Country Club for a round of golf.[122] A friendship grew and Graham would often visit with Nixon when he was in Washington. In 1957 Nixon represented Eisenhower at the Yankee Stadium climax to the New York City Crusade and told the huge crowd how deeply moved he was to be present. Though he was heavily pressed to endorse Nixon in 1960, Graham kept his silence.

Between 1960 and 1967 the two men kept in touch, often golfing together in California or Florida and occasionally dining together when Graham came to New York where Nixon later practiced law. In December of 1967 Graham, though convalescing from pneumonia, was asked by Nixon to come to Key Biscayne to discuss Nixon's course of action in the race for the Republican nomination in the upcoming Presidential election. Nixon later described the experience for *Good Housekeeping* magazine: "We took long walks on the beach, talking. In the end I decided that if they really wanted me, it would be worth all the hell. Billy Graham had a great deal to do with that decision." [123] Perhaps so, but Nixon had been carefully laying plans for capturing the nomination long before the December walks on the beach with Graham. At any rate he lost few opportunities throughout the campaign to relate the crucial role Graham had played in bringing him into the fray.

Early in the summer Graham began to feel the familiar pressures of 1960 and 1964. His position was again to not publicly endorse a candidate. He would however "use his influence as much as possible with both major parties to assure candidates of moral and spiritual values." [124] The first real indication that this was going to be a different kind of campaign for Graham came at the Republican convention when in the hours immediately after Nixon's nomination he met with the candidate and key Republican leaders to discuss the Vice Presidential nomination. Graham later told Edward Fiske that Nixon asked for his preference, and he had replied that Senator Hatfield would "give balance to your ticket. First of all he's a great Christian leader. He's almost a clergyman. He's been an educator and has taken a more liberal stance on most issues than you, and I think the ticket needs that kind of a balance." [125] In retrospect this seems like an excellent abstract analysis which did not take into account certain political realities pressing Nixon. One of these realities was Hatfield's support of the Arab cause in the Middle East crisis, a stance which differs from the position held by Graham and most of the Middle America constituency which has been so vital to Nixon.[126]

Just a few days after Nixon's nomination Graham felt compelled to inform his followers that he would remain neutral in the campaign. Thus, on August 18, he mailed a letter from his Minneapolis headquarters saying that he would take the advice of "his friends Nixon and Johnson" and stay out of politics. The communication, however, led some to suggest that in actuality Graham was endorsing the Republican candidate. This conclusion was drawn from the following portion of the letter. "Naturally my convictions and sympathies are strong this year and it will be difficult to keep quiet when I feel so deeply! However, I am praying that the man of God's choice will be elected." [127] In September Graham and Nixon appeared together but this time, unlike the 1960 experience when Graham attended a Nixon rally, Nixon attended a Graham crusade. The Republican candidate and his wife came to the concluding service of the Pittsburgh Crusade on the eleventh.[128] Graham introduced the Nixons, who were sitting in the middle of the audience, and described his friendship with the candidate as "one of the most cherished I have ever had with anyone." He then went on to praise Nixon for his "generosity, tremendous constraint of temper, and his integrity in totaling his golf score." Graham concluded by asking the crowd "whether Republican or

Democrat to extend a warm welcome to the Nixons." After the service Nixon told newsmen, "this was one of the most moving religious experiences of my life." [129] Lest this sound overly partisan, Graham read to the audience a wire received just prior to the meeting from Hubert Humphrey. The Democratic hopeful expressed deep admiration for Graham's work and congratulated the evangelist on the Pittsburgh Crusade's "great success." [130] Humphrey might not have had a Jim Wine on his team but at least he was trying.

The impression felt by many that Graham had indeed endorsed Nixon was expressed in a unique manner by an American Baptist editor, Norman R. DePuy. Writing in the October issue of *Mission,* DePuy commended Graham for his courage in "taking sides in the Presidential election." [131] If Graham had not publicly endorsed the Republican standard bearer he was given new opportunity to come very close to an endorsement by former Undersecretary of State George Ball who early in October questioned Nixon's integrity. On October 16 Graham issued a statement attacking Ball for reflecting on Nixon's "moral character and personal integrity." [132] He added, "I can testify that he is a man of high moral principles. I do not intend publicly to endorse any political candidate as some clergymen are doing but I maintain the right to help put the record straight when a friend is smeared." Graham, who several times during the campaign used the word "change" to describe the mood of the American people, then said, that his "fellow citizens were looking for a change in the moral and spiritual direction of the nation and that candidates for President should be aware of that fact." [133] This statement, which received wide attention in the press, could not have failed to help Nixon, who throughout the campaign stressed his friendship with Graham. On the other hand a strong case can be made that, friendship aside, Nixon was the kind of candidate Graham genuinely thought was needed at this particular juncture in American life. *Time* magazine, in an analysis of Graham's political thought, suggested its affinity to Nixon's key positions:

> Like Nixon, Graham considers that the Supreme Court has "gone too far" in favoring criminals. He supports Black Power, but only if it means "a feeling of self respect," not violence or civil disobedience. He believes that the demonstrators at the Democratic Convention in Chicago were "wonderful kids, idealists—but manipulated by a small, well-organized hard core that wanted a confrontation." The Chicago police overreacted but "I don't know how some of the policemen restrained themselves that long." [134]

It is obvious that such views are most representative of Middle America, which today forms the most significant bloc of each man's constituency.

Immediately after the election Graham was asked to comment on Nixon's religious views. Speaking on the CBS radio program, World of Religion, Graham said that Nixon's "deep religious roots will be a factor as in the Kennedy administration, that of Eisenhower and that of Johnson, each had deep religious roots." [135] In a more specific sense Graham praised Nixon:

> He has a great sense of moral integrity. I think he will be a respected President because I think that it will come across to the American people. But I have never seen any indication of or agreed with the label that his enemies have given him of "tricky Dick." In the years I've known him, he's never given any indication of being tricky.[136]

Calling upon his knowledge of the President-elect's mother, Graham concluded:

> Mr. Nixon has a deep religious past. His mother was deeply religious. I participated last summer in her funeral and, listening to the statements of her friends and from my knowledge of her, she can be said to have been deeply religious—and this will have a bearing on President Nixon. *I'd hate to see a man who didn't believe in God, one who didn't have a religious faith, in the White House. I think it would be a disaster.*[137] (Italics added.)

The Nixon–Graham Doctrine

A few months later Graham outlined his expectations concerning the practical aspect of the Nixon Presidency. Speaking on the World of Religion, April 1, 1969, he said: "The pattern of the Nixon Administration will probably be partially based on what Mr. Nixon has learned as an understudy of Eisenhower. I believe Mr. Eisenhower's life made a great impact on Mr. Nixon as a young man." [138] That Graham had great hopes for the new Administration was apparent on Inauguration Day when in his 600-word prayer he gave thanks that "in thy sovereignty Thou hast permitted Richard Nixon to lead us at this momentous hour of history." [139]

By the end of January 1969 the effects of the relationship of the two men upon the course of government was already being widely discussed. On January 31 *Life* Magazine editorialized that "the White House atmosphere will be in part one of deliberate reflection. But the omnipresence of evangelist Billy Graham means that the idealism which will emerge is bound to have the urgency and the overtones of evangelism." [140] Obviously not everyone was pleased by this possibility and the views of many thoughtful liberal Christians were expressed by famed theologian Reinhold Niebuhr who, in *Christianity and Crisis,* attacked the "Nixon-Graham doctrine" which suggests that a spiritual solution must be found for current American problems. Niebuhr also criticized Graham for his undue confidence in individual conversion which "obscures the dual individual and social character of human selves and the individual and social character of their virtues and vices." [141] Later in the Administration Will Campbell, a Baptist minister and former official of the NCC, would characterize Graham as "a false court prophet who tells Nixon and the Pentagon what they want to hear." [142]

If the public could not know just how the relationship between Graham and Nixon affected national life they were constantly reminded that the relationship existed and apparently deepened. When the President instituted religious services in the White House, Graham was the first speaker and thus far has been the only preacher to be invited for a repeat appearance. Graham also was the speaker at the 1969 annual Presidential Prayer Breakfast, the first in the series to be held in the White House. The frequency with which the two men were together can be measured by Graham's date book for three weeks in September 1969, during which period Graham flew to the Pacific Coast three times: 1) to accept an invitation from Nixon to be one of two clergymen present at the dinner for the moon astronauts, 2) to take part in a meeting of the Richard Nixon Foundation of which he is a board member, and 3) to join the President for a round of activities which included a flight on Air Force One to the Redlands dedication honoring Lady Bird Johnson, several games of golf with the President, and a stay at the Western White House.[143]

Two events in 1970 appeared to link Graham even more closely to the Nixon Administration. In both instances, Nixon was accused of using his friendship with Graham for political purposes. On Thursday, May 28, Nixon flew to Knoxville to appear with Graham at a religious service in Volunteer Stadium on the University of Tennessee campus.[144] Nixon not only brought greetings and praised Graham: "all men share respect for the message he brings because what he will say to you is what America and the world needs to hear," [145] but made a lengthy address directed at youth and defending his record as President. Seated on the platform along with local religious leaders, was Republican senatorial candidate William E. Brock III, locked at that time in a fierce campaign with the incumbent Democratic Senator, Albert Gore. Gore was conspicuous by his absence. Since Republican strategists had seen Gore's seat as the most desirable to pick up in the new Congress, observers could not help viewing the service as a GOP political rally. Questioned after the meeting Graham said that the only person he had invited was Nixon and as far as he was concerned anyone in Tennessee could have come. He added, "This is not a Presidential election year. He is the President of all of the people. There were no political implications. If I thought there were I would not have invited him." [146] The rally produced continuing headlines. Graham, whose usual practice is to have local politicians as platform guests, should have been more careful knowing that Nixon was coming to Tennessee during a torrid political race. It is unfortunate that the incident and the accompanying antiwar demonstration aimed at Nixon marred what was otherwise a highly successful crusade. One of the authors was present a few days earlier and was most impressed with Graham's stress on amelioration of social ills. When the evangelist turned to the hundreds who had come forward to receive Christ, his first words were a challenge to "return to the office, shop or school and love the person of another race." [147] These words, coming in a state which gave a significant share of its vote to George Wallace two years earlier, were indeed impressive.

Honor America Day

The second event in 1970 in which it appeared that Nixon was taking advantage of his friendship with Graham was the Honor America Day observance on the Fourth of July. Graham claimed the concept emerged from a conversation he had had with Hobart Lewis, president of *Reader's Digest*. After discussing recent student demonstrations and racial unrest, the two men agreed that it would be good to "try to get everybody together and say 'we believe in the institutions of America.' " [148] Lewis asked Graham if he would be willing to work with Bob Hope in putting a program together. Graham called Hope and after being assured of the comedian's support, told him, "Let's keep it away from the war. This is not pro-war or anti-war. Let's make it for all America." [149] Graham had taken an ambivalent position on the war since the Johnson era. At first he supported the United States effort and at one point visited Southeast Asia as an unofficial Johnson emissary.[150] Later he returned to Vietnam and along with Cardinal Spellman of New York conducted religious services for the troops. Spellman, who was clearly a hawk, tried but did not succeed in converting Graham to his position. Graham did come out strongly against dissent in 1967. He warned that antiwar protests "so exaggerate our divisions over the war that they could make Hanoi confident it will eventually win." [151] A year later he changed his position somewhat and admitted to bafflement on the war. "I sometimes think we tend to blame America too much and the Viet Cong too little, but I wonder about the advisability of Americanizing the war. My only hope is that we will end it." [152] By 1970 Graham was more disturbed with what he considered to be the by-products of the war than with the actual fighting itself, which seemed finally to be winding down. In Graham's eyes the war and its resultant internal argumentation and dissent had seriously weakened the nation. On the eve of the New York City Crusade in June the evangelist stated that the war had also "opened the way for extremists to seize upon the flag and traditional American values and make them their own. We have allowed the word 'patriotism' to get into the hands of some right wingers." [153] He then called for more confidence in American political institutions, asserting that the flag, for example, was the property of all Americans. In a comment which graphically indicated how far his position was from the Christian right he said: "I don't guess anybody loves the flag more than some of the people that are against the war." [154] Honor America Day was an attempt to bring together pro- and antiwar forces in a celebration of the traditional America. What Graham, Hope and Lewis did not anticipate was that the antiwar elements would not join in the festivities. Indeed these groups picketed the program and harassed the participants throughout the day. (When the morning religious service ended, one of the authors was riding in a car to Washington's National Airport with participants Astronaut Frank Borman and Bishop Fulton J. Sheen. He was shocked to hear young people shout obscenities at the two men as the limousine slowed for a curve.) [155]

What Graham and his Honor America Day associates did clearly see was a developing trend in American life which favored ending the war and establishing reconciliation between conflicting forces. The polls indicated that Middle America was rapidly moving toward this position, but the antiwar militants were as out of tune with the real meaning of this trend as were Carl McIntire and Billy James Hargis, who still beat the bushes for subversives and traitors. Graham was responsible for organizing and providing the personnel for the morning religious service. Hope produced the entertainment extravaganza scheduled for the evening. In addition, Graham gave the principal address at the morning ceremony. This address merits careful study, for in a genuine sense it is a valedictory statement made by the religious leader of the new American majority. Standing before the Lincoln Memorial on a mercilessly hot Washington summer morning, Graham outlined his vision of what America means and should be.

Graham's speech, "The Unfinished Dream," took as its text I Peter 2:17: "Honor all men. . . . Fear God. Honor the King." Graham interpreted this last phrase in the context of a republic to mean "honor the nation." Not only, he claimed, were the thousands gathered to honor the nation, but also to "renew our dedication and allegiance to the principles and institutions which made her great. Lately our institutions have been under attack: the Supreme Court, the Congress, the Presidency, the flag, the home, the educational system, and even the church—but we are here to say with loud voices that in spite of their faults and failures we believe in these institutions!" [156]

Graham then dealt with what he believed to be the chief cause of trouble in American society—the activity of extremists. "There is too much discouragement, despair and negativism in the nation today. On every hand critics tell us what is wrong with America, where we have failed and why we are hated. We have listened and watched while a relatively small extremist element both to the left and the right in our society have [*sic*] knocked our courts, desecrated our flag, disrupted our educational system, laughed at our religious heritage and threatened to burn down our cities—and are now threatening to assassinate our leaders." Graham correctly ascribed the reactions of the American center to these factors: "The overwhelming majority of concerned Americans—white and black, hawks and doves, parents and students, Republicans and Democrats—who hate violence have stood by and viewed all this with mounting alarm and concern. Today we call upon all Americans to stop this polarization before it is too late."

Graham then turned to the question as to why as a Christian minister he should "join in honoring any secular state." Three Biblical quotations provided an answer: 1) Jesus saying to render unto Caesar the things that are Caesar's; 2) the Apostle Paul boasting of his Roman citizenship, and 3) the phrase "Honor the nation." Yet Graham would not necessarily feel the same about any other nation. America because of her unique past, her system of government and her promise for the future deserved honor and respect from the Christian who straddles two worlds. In addition, those who practice other religions as well as atheists have a responsibility to "an America that has always stood for liberty, protection and opportunity." Graham went on to enumerate seven reasons why America should be honored just six years from her two hundredth birthday: 1) she has opened her doors to the distressed; 2) she has been the most generous nation in history; 3) she has never hidden her problems and faults; 4) she is honestly recognizing and is courageously trying to solve her social problems; 5) she has never sought to use her tremendous power to take over other nations; 6) she defends the right of her citizens to dissent; 7) there is "woven into the warp and woof of our nation faith in God." These seven points are an almost classic incantation of all that is good with America, the past that one can point to with pride, the present that one can examine with confidence, the future that one can look to with hope.

Graham up to this part of his address had spoken in the classic tradition of Fourth of July oratory. One major difference between him and thousands of predecessors on uncounted village greens was that he addressed a nationwide television audience over three major networks who had preempted their regular programming in order to carry his remarks. Graham next turned to the litany of problems currently disturbing America: racism, poverty, pollution, moral permissiveness, an excess of freedom which borders on license, alcohol, drugs, illicit sex, pornography, religious occultism, and the searching questions posed by youth to elders who too often have no answers. All these, he declared, threaten the peace and stability of our society.

Not surprisingly, Graham saw a remedy in spiritual revival. For the Bible teaches that "God will judge any nation that turns its back on Him—especially a nation like America which has been given more privileges and opportunities than any nation in history." Graham recalled that Eisenhower at his first inauguration "put his finger on a verse that every American should remember today." The verse, supplied to the general when he asked Graham for a fitting Scripture quotation to use in his inaugural address, was from the Old Testament (2 Chronicles 7:14): "If my people, which are called by my name, shall humble themselves, and pray, and seek my face, and turn from their wicked ways; then will I hear from heaven, and will forgive their sin, and will heal their land." Graham then called "upon all Americans to raise voices in prayer and dedication to God and recommitment to the ideals and dreams upon which our country was founded." He exhorted his hearers, "Let's dedicate ourselves to a renewal of faith in God, equality, justice and peace for all. Let's dedicate ourselves to building rather than burning. I am asking all Americans today, especially our young people, to pursue this vision under God, to work for freedom and peace, to labor relentlessly, to love passionately, to serve selflessly, to pray earnestly, and to die nobly if need be. I say to you today: Pursue the vision, teach toward the goal, fulfill the dream and as you move to do it, never give in! Never give in!"

When Honor America Day ended with the Hope show and the greatest fireworks display in the history of the capital, some analysts saw an important net gain for Nixon. The President did not appear. In fact, he spent the holiday at San Clemente but the shadow of his presence loomed large. The observance seemed to echo some of the major themes of the Nixon Administration: that the country could right itself if only political unity, personal dedication, and moderateness of language and action prevailed. The suspicion that Nixon strongly approved of Honor America Day was confirmed in the personal letter he sent to each of the major participants. Yet Graham in his remarks was not shilling for Nixon, or even trying to aid his good friend in a deeply troubled period. He was being true to himself and his own moral and spiritual commitment. In a larger sense he was saying to Nixon and other potential seekers of the office Nixon held that his particular prescription of patriotism combined with moderateness and spirituality was the panacea for America's ills. If anything the Honor America speech moved Graham more firmly than ever into the broad and politically decisive center of the nation's life. The screaming young people in the wading pool in front of the Lincoln Memorial and the placard-waving McIntire supporters at the fringe of the crowd were more than made up for by the plaudits of main-street America. Graham was suggesting a way out of the wilderness, a path not like the straight and narrow where Southern strategies and Northeastern radicalism could prosper, but the broad path which could lead in 1972 to political success if those who have ears to hear would pause to listen.

BILLY GRAHAM: AN EVALUATION

Over ten years ago, distinguished historian of American religion William G. McLoughlin declared that Billy Graham had reached the peak of his career and would soon step down as a great revivalist in the tradition of Charles Finney, Dwight L. Moody and Billy Sunday. McLoughlin suggested that Graham's "anti-intellectualism and individualistic emphasis" would ill-fit him for leadership in a time when Protestant theology was undergoing a reorientation away from the older liberalism.[157] McLoughlin rightly saw that the theological and ecclesiastical aspects of the awakening precipitated by Graham's ministry would take place within the organized churches, but he did not correctly see that this new revival would bypass the leaders of the National and World Councils of Churches. Similarly his prediction that the National Association of Evangelicals would wither also was flawed. What McLoughlin could not know in 1960 was that Graham and many of the other evangelical leaders had the capacity to learn, grow and widen their ministries without compromising their basic spiritual and moral commitments. Nor could he know that a new majority of Christians, cutting across denominational lines, would look increasingly to Graham for leadership on social and political issues as well as in theological matters.

The events of the sixties and the development of the new social class known as Middle America have made Graham's career a continuing success story. Another estimate of the evangelist, articulated even earlier by a leading rabbi, was both perceptive and prophetic. After attending several meetings of the 1957 New York Crusade, Herbert Weiner, writing in *Commentary,* described Graham's ministry as "a peculiarly American brand of evangelism . . . an evangelism eager above all to be popular. It seeks the friendship of all political parties, supports all churches, bids for the good will of intellectuals and refuses to have anything to do with bigotry. It holds out the possibility of a deep religious experience, it provides a simple answer to all problems, with the assurance that surrender will not affect the convert's status in the community, indeed, will not even make him lose his friends in the crowd. It is . . . evangelism made respectable." [158]

Not everyone would agree that the message of Billy Graham

is really adequate for the future, however respectable the evangelist may have made it. Thus, John C. Bennett, former president of Union Theological Seminary (New York) and a leading Protestant social ethicist, says of Billy Graham:

> He can denounce war in general, corruption, the drug culture, the preoccupation with sex, racial discrimination, and all manifestations of greed, and yet what he says will not trouble the powers most responsible for these evils. . . . He has a *personal* message that may help *individuals* to live free of *private* burdens of sin and guilt and aimlessness, but he lets down those who see themselves as the victims of institutionalized injustice and those who are outraged by many acts of their Government abroad.[159] [Italics added.]

At the recent Oakland Crusade, Graham urged the members of the burgeoning "Jesus people" or "Jesus freak" movement to avoid politics and to devote their energies to the proclamation of the gospel of personal redemption. Bennett comments:

> All of this is strange talk from the man who has allowed himself to be used by two Presidents to give moral and religious sanction to their politics. . . . When people claim to be above politics it is axiomatic that they in effect support the status quo. This is true when they do nothing, but it is far more true when they advertise their close relations with the powerful.[160]

Nevertheless, by 1971 most American Christians touched by this evangelism would agree with John Connally's description of the role Graham plays in contemporary society: "Billy Graham is more than a preacher, more than an evangelist, more than a Christian leader. In a greater sense he has become our conscience."[161] It might be added that the elevation of Graham to the role of national conscience in the early 1970's is not only fitting but also much healthier than many other paradigms which have been paraded before the public by the news media, interest groups, and some religious bodies. In a day of instant and easily deflatable heroes, Graham's longevity as a deeply respected person of stature is nothing short of amazing. In his active ministry Graham has done well by the New Testament injunction that to whom much is given much is expected. He has had opportunities for travel, learning and association with the influential unparalleled in the life of any other past or present evangelical leader. Through it all, however, he has still remained faithful to his calling. He has remained a warm and truly authentic human being and a faithful steward of the gifts granted him. He has come much further along the paths of tolerance and understanding than most of his contemporaries in evangelicalism and, despite criticism from the extremes, has made fundamentalist Christianity respectable and even desirable. In response to a recent question on what the future of this Christianity might be, he replied:

> I have very strong hope for the future of evangelical Christianity in America. It has been in the history of the evangelical movement that it has had its times of difficulty and recession but it always has responded in critical times and the work has gone on. There has been quite a noticeable trend in the last few years of a growing evangelical force in America and there seems to be no reason to anticipate a recession at least at the present time.[162]

His vision is shared by not only the 31,000,000 conservative Protestants in America but also by other millions who act to form the new American majority. His feet may be planted in the world of the spiritual rather than the secular but his prognosis for America is, to the politically decisive bulk of its inhabitants, the timeliest compilation of all they hope for and all they fear. Speaking at the National Press Club on December 19, 1969, Graham voiced his prescription for America's future well-being in these words:

> What we need most in America today is a revitalization of Judeo-Christianity. We must have a renewal of faith in God, faith in one another, faith in everything our country is supposed to stand for. Without that renewal, without a revitalization of the church, the educational system, the government

structure and the mass media, our national survival as a free democracy seems to be improbable.[163]

NOTES

1. Religious News Service 7/30/70. In succeeding notes references to this source will be abbreviated as RNS.
2. RNS 9/30/70.
3. Report of Gallup Poll findings in RNS 1/15/69.
4. Clarence Mitchell, *Billy Graham: The Making of a Crusader* (Philadelphia and New York: Chilton Books, 1966), p. 91.
5. John Pollock, *Billy Graham: The Authorized Biography* (New York: McGraw-Hill Book Company, 1966), page 25, note 1.
6. *Ibid.*, p. 32.
7. *Ibid.*, p. 53.
8. John Pollock, *Crusades: 20 Years with Billy Graham* (Minneapolis: World Wide Publications, 1969), p. 64. This is an updated version of *Billy Graham: The Authorized Biography* and places special stress on the Graham mass crusades.
9. *Ibid.*, p. 70.
10. Ockenga is currently President of Gordon College and Divinity School of which Graham is a board member.
11. The governor was J. Strom Thurmond, now a Senator from South Carolina. Ten years later Governor Bell Timmerman, Jr. would bar Graham from the State House grounds because the evangelist was "a widely known advocate of desegregation."
12. Pollock, *Crusades*, p. 75.
13. Joshua Loth Liebman, *Peace of Mind* (New York: Simon and Schuster, 1946); Fulton J. Sheen, *Peace of Soul* (New York: Doubleday and Company, 1954); Norman Vincent Peale, *The Power of Positive Thinking* (New York: Prentice-Hall, 1952).
14. See Carl F. H. Henry, *The Uneasy Conscience of Modern Fundamentalism* (Grand Rapids, Mich.: Wm B. Eerdmans Company, 1947); *Protestant Dilemma* (Grand Rapids, Mich.: William B. Eerdmans Company, 1948); Edward John Carnell, *Introduction to Christian Apologetics* (Grand Rapids, Mich.: William B. Eerdmans Company, 1948).
15. John Corry, "God, Country and Billy Graham," *Harper's Magazine*, February, 1969, p. 36.
16. Pollock, *Crusades*, p. 141.
17. RNS 4/2/69.
18. RNS 7/15/68.
19. *The Lamp*, October, 1969, p. 10; RNS 10/2/68. In November 1963 Graham addressed 1500 students and priests at Belmont Abbey College, Belmont, N.C. He described the experience as "a very important part of my ministerial career." In response, The Very Rev. John Noetgen, President of the Abbey, told the audience that the college had been praised for being the first Catholic institution to invite Graham to speak. He added, "After hearing your talk we should be blamed for having waited so long." (RNS 11/21/63) The following year Graham visited Richard Cardinal Cushing at the Archbishop's

Boston residence. Cushing urged Catholics to attend the Graham Boston crusade and commented "I only wish we had a half dozen of his caliber to go forth and preach the gospel." (RNS 10/7/64) Speaking in San Antonio in June 1968 Graham described the support Roman Catholics were giving to his work. He said, "A great part of our support comes from Catholics. We never hold a crusade without priests and nuns being very much in evidence in the audience." (RNS 6/24/68)

20. New York *Times,* June 1, 1970, p. 15.
21. Typescript of New York radio station WINS Religion Commentary "Billy Graham and Jewish Community," broadcast on May 31, 1970.
22. Copy of statement released by Dr. Graham's Minneapolis office on May 25, 1971; see also Jewish Telegraphic Agency, 5/25/71.
23. Chicago *Sun-Times,* 6/12/71, p. 40.
24. RNS 5/29/69.
25. World of Religion broadcast. See RNS 12/6/68.
26. RNS 12/14/70.
27. RNS 6/20/69.
28. Chicago *Sun-Times,* 6/12/71, p. 40.
29. *Ibid.,* p. 40.
30. See Chapter 3.
31. Billy Graham, *World Aflame* (Garden City, N.Y.: Doubleday and Company, Inc., 1965), p. 70.
32. *Ibid.,* p. 71.
33. *Ibid.,* p. 73.
34. *Ibid.,* p. 78.
35. *Ibid.,* p. 79.
36. 2 Cor. 5:17.
37. Graham, *op. cit.,* p. 124.
38. *Ibid.,* p. 203.
39. *Ibid.,* pp. 216–229.
40. RNS 6/10/68.
41. Carl F. H. Henry, "Evangelicals in the Social Struggle," *Christianity Today,* October 8, 1965, pp. 3–11.
42. Galatians 5:22.
43. "I have been crucified with Christ; it is no longer I who live but Christ who lives in me; and the life I now live in the flesh I live by faith in the Son of God who loved me and gave himself for me." (RSV)
44. J. Archie Hargraves, "Go Where the Action Is: The Church and Urbanization," *Social Action,* February, 1964, pp. 15–35.
45. See Chapter 3.
46. Letter to Authors, August 13, 1971.
47. *Christianity Today,* January 19, 1968, p. 5.
48. RNS 12/22/64.
49. RNS 1/10/68.
50. *Ibid.*
51. New York *Times,* December 6, 1966, p. 38.
52. *Ibid.*
53. RNS 4/23/71.
54. RNS 2/18/71.
55. Notes related to visit to Interchurch Center, June 1969.
56. *Reader's Digest,* August, 1960, p. 56.

57. *Ibid.*
58. New York *Times,* May 18, 1961, p. 26.
59. New York *Times,* 5/18/63, p. 21.
60. RNS 4/25/63.
61. There are conflicting estimates of the crowd. RNS reported 50,000, while the New York *Times'* estimate was "more than 35,000."
62. New York *Times,* March 30, 1964, p. 1.
63. RNS 3/30/64.
64. RNS 3/30/64.
65. RNS 4/8/64.
66. RNS 4/9/64.
67. New York *Times,* May 18, 1964, p. 25.
68. RNS 6/9/64.
69. *Ibid.*
70. RNS 9/3/64. Earlier that year Graham told a group of religious leaders in Boston, "In the South there is real friendship upon which to build a solution to the problem. In the North you have de facto segregation and this is much harder to overcome." (RNS 2/20/64.) See also the New York *Times* of April 17, 1965, p. 8.
71. RNS 3/3/65.
72. New York *Times,* March 13, 1965, p. 60.
73. New York *Times,* April 5, 1965, p. 37.
74. New York *Times,* April 17, 1965, p. 8.
75. *Ibid.*
76. RNS 4/28/65.
77. *Ibid.*
78. New York *Times,* April 26, 1965, p. 34.
79. RNS 6/18/65.
80. New York *Times,* June 21, 1965, p. 15.
81. *Ibid.*
82. New York *Times,* August 16, 1965, p. 18.
83. *Ibid.*
84. RNS 8/27/65.
85. *Ibid.*
86. See David Lawrence, "Billy Graham's Plea to President Johnson," *U.S. News and World Report,* August 7, 1967, p. 92.
87. *Ibid.*
88. See RNS 8/3/67.
89. *Ibid.*
90. January 6, 1971.
91. RNS 3/16/70.
92. Letter to Authors, August 13, 1971.
93. June 16, 1971.
94. RNS 11/23/70.
95. In the fall of 1970 Graham made several one-minute TV spot announcements urging compliance with school integration legislation. These announcements were broadcast in his home state of North Carolina. (RNS 9/8/70)
96. Quoted by John Cogley, New York *Times,* September 4, 1966, Section E., p. 12.
97. See issues of the *Western Voice* and *Christian Beacon,* Summer, Fall, 1960.
98. On April 29, 1960, delegates to the annual meeting of the NAE ex-

pressed doubt that a Roman Catholic President "could or would resist fully the pressures of the ecclesiastical hierarchy."

99. *Christianity Today,* February 1, 1960, p. 20; June 20, 1960, p. 31; October 24, 1960, p. 25; October 26, 1969, pp. 22–23.
100. See Patricia Barrett, "Religion and the 1960 Presidential Election" *Social Order,* June, 1962.
101. Edward Fiske, "The Closest Thing to a White House Chaplain," *New York Times Magazine,* June 8, 1969, p. 114.
102. New York *Herald Tribune,* January 17, 1961.
103. New York *Times,* January 17, 1961, p. 24.
104. New York *Herald Tribune,* January 17, 1961.
105. *Ibid.*
106. RNS 10/23/62.
107. RNS 5/23/62.
108. Washington *Post,* March 25, 1962.
109. RNS 8/30/63.
110. *Ibid.* In later years Graham would support a program Shriver headed. On June 15, 1967 he told a group of Congressional and business leaders that he was "a convert" to the war on poverty. He added, "This is the first time in seventeen years I have come to Washington to speak for or against a government program." (RNS 6/16/71)
111. RNS 4/12/65.
112. *Ibid.*
113. New York *Times,* November 3, 1964, p. 23.
114. RNS 9/3/64.
115. RNS 4/12/65.
116. New York *Journal American,* November 5, 1965, p. 27.
117. *Christianity Today,* December 17, 1965, p. 33.
118. Fiske, *op. cit.,* p. 108.
119. Pollock, *Crusades,* p. 285.
120. Wesley Pippert, "Billy Graham: Prophet or Politician," *Christian Life,* May 1971, p. 54.
121. *Ibid.*
122. *Ibid.*
123. *Good Housekeeping,* July 1968.
124. RNS 8/12/68.
125. Fiske, *New York Times Magazine,* According to RNS 8/12/68 Graham personally gave Hatfield the word that he would not be the nominee.
126. See *Baptist Press,* November 17, 1970, p. 3, for results of Southern Baptist View Poll.
127. RNS 8/19/68.
128. RNS 9/12/68.
129. *Ibid.*
130. *Ibid.*
131. *Mission,* October, 1968, p. 21.
132. RNS 10/16/68.
133. *Ibid.*
134. *Time,* October 4, 1968, p. 58.
135. RNS 11/11/68.
136. *Ibid.*
137. *Ibid.*
138. World of Religion. See RNS 4/2/69.

139. *Congressional Record,* January 20, 1969, S561.
140. *Life,* January 31, 1969.
141. Reinhold Niebuhr, "The King's Chapel and the King's Court," *Christianity and Crisis,* August 4, 1969, pp. 211–212.
142. See RNS 3/12/71.
143. RNS 9/10/69.
144. New York *Times,* May 29, 1970, p. 1.
145. See transcript of Nixon's remarks. *Ibid.,* p. 8.
146. Pippert, *op. cit.,* p. 29.
147. Notes taken May 25, 1970.
148. New York *Times,* June 24, 1970, p. 37.
149. *Ibid.*
150. RNS 5/22/67.
151. See "Graham Denounces Dissenters," *Christian Century,* May 17, 1967, p. 645.
152. *Newsweek,* June 10, 1963, p. 63.
153. New York *Times,* June 24, 1970, p. 37.
154. *Ibid.*
155. Notes July 4, 1970.
156. All quotations from the Honor America Day speech are from mimeographed version given to the press on the morning of July 4, 1970.
157. William G. McLoughlin, Jr., *Billy Graham: Revivalist in a Secular Age* (New York: The Ronald Press Company, 1960), p. 230–231.
158. Herbert Weiner, "Billy Graham: Respectable Evangelism," *Commentary,* September 1957, pp. 257–262.
159. "Billy Graham in Oakland," *Christianity and Crisis,* October 4, 1971, p. 196.
160. *Ibid.*
161. Quoted in Pollock, *Crusades,* p. 282.
162. Letter to authors, August 13, 1971.
163. *Christianity Today,* December 19, 1969, p. 262. Graham had earlier stressed this theme on September 22, 1969 at the first Presidential Prayer Breakfast to be held in the White House: "I think the greatest need in America at this moment is a spiritual revival . . . unless we turn to God as Washington and Lincoln did I must confess to you that I fear for the future of the country." (RNS 9/22/69)

3

Fundamentalism—The Faith of Billy Graham

The world longs for authority, finality, and conclusiveness. It is weary of theological floundering and uncertainty. Belief exhilarates the human spirit; doubt depresses . . .[1]

Just before the first tent meetings in Los Angeles I became absolutely convinced that the Bible was the Word of God. Today my convictions concerning the Bible are much stronger. I have seen the Word of God penetrate the hearts of people and transform and change them. I know that this Book was inspired by the Holy Spirit. It is a supernatural book. This is a Living Word.

The events we see happening in our world today are the fulfillment of prophecies made centuries ago by the prophets of Israel, by Jesus Christ Himself, and the apostles. Everything is falling into position with almost frightening precision. Prophecy is being fulfilled to the letter . . .

We do not know the day nor the hour that our Lord is to return, but we are told to watch the signs. They are all pointing in one direction, the soon coming of the Lord Jesus Christ. . . . If ever there was an hour when you needed to repent and believe and make sure of your personal relationship with God, it is now.[2]

Personal transformation, the final authority of the divinely inspired Word of God, the imminence of the Second Coming of the Lord Jesus Christ, belief which exhilarates the human spirit—for more than twenty years this has been the message of Billy Graham. But as modern as his methods have been, as distinctive as the personality of the preacher remains, there is nothing new or startling in the message of Billy Graham. For America has heard this message in every generation since the mid-eighteenth century. In the twentieth century we have grown accustomed to calling this gospel by a name born of religious controversy: *Fundamentalism.* In the present chapter, we turn our attention from the career of America's most enduring hero to the content of his faith, a faith which he shares with an ever more influential segment of the American population.

What is fundamentalism? A movement? A mentality? A creed? A way of life? Or all of the above?

According to the *Oxford English Dictionary,* fundamentalism is "a religious *movement* which became active among various Protestant bodies in the United States after the war of 1914–18, based on strict adherence to traditional tenets (e.g. the literal inerrancy of Scripture) held to be fundamental to the Christian faith: opposed to *liberalism* and *modernism.*" The *Concise Oxford Dictionary* emphasizes the attitudinal aspect, defining fundamentalism as "the *maintenance,* in opposition to modernism, of traditional orthodox beliefs such as the inerrancy of Scripture and literal acceptance of the creeds as fundamentals of Protestant Christianity." L. Harold DeWolf, in *Present Trends in Christian Thought,* lays stress to the essentially polemic character of fundamentalism, explaining it as "an effort to reaffirm the fundamentals of the Christian faith, in *vigorous reaction and protest* against liberal theology." On the other hand, expressing his alarm with a mentality and a way of life which the fundamentalist protests have produced, Edward John Carnell pithily declares: *"Fundamentalism is orthodoxy gone cultic."* [3]

The word *fundamentalist* was born of controversy, the

battle between the forces of "old-style" Christian orthodoxy and "newfangled" religious and social notions known collectively as *modernism*. The years of struggle were 1918 to 1931. The issue best known to the public at large was evolution. The most illustrious fundamentalist of these years was William Jennings Bryan, the thrice-defeated Presidential candidate who aided in the prosecution of John Thomas Scopes, the young teacher accused of violating the Tennessee Anti-Evolution Act of 1925. But behind the fundamentalist controversy lay the fundamentalist movement, and a religious dispute between theological positions which divided Protestant Christianity.

On the one side stood the modernists. "What then is modernism?" asked Shailer Mathews, dean of the Divinity School of the University of Chicago. In a 1924 essay, *The Faith of Modernism,* he explained:

> *It is the use of the methods of modern science to find, state, and use the permanent and central values of inherited orthodoxy in meeting the needs of a modern world.* . . . The modernist movement is a phase of the scientific struggle for freedom in thought and belief. . . . Modernists are Christians who accept the results of scientific research as data with which to think religiously. . . . Modernists are Christians who adopt the methods of historical and literary science in the study of the Bible and religion. . . . The modernist Christian believes the Christian religion will help men meet social as well as individual needs. . . . The modernist is a Christian who believes that the spiritual and moral needs of the world can be met because they are intellectually convinced that Christian attitudes and faiths are consistent with other realities. . . . Modernists as a class are evangelical Christians. That is, they accept Jesus Christ as the revelation of a Savior God.[4]

In a more extreme form, a modernist might hold to the sort of "liberal" credo ascribed to a young minister in Luther Little's fundamentalist novel, *Manse-Dwellers* (1927):

> Jesus was born of a human father and mother. He was divine only as are other men. He was the greatest of prophets

> and ethical teachers. He attained the highest degree of trust in God. We are to imitate his religious life. He is himself not the object of religious trust and worship. His recorded miracles are mainly myth and fiction, the imaginings of fond disciples. In some cases of healing he exerted a kind of magnetic power, such as we often observe today in so-called "divine healers." There was no real resurrection and ascension. There was, doubtless, belief in the resurrection, but it was based on manifestations like those of modern spiritualism. They are simply psychic phenomena of the subjective kind. There was no objective ground of forgiveness in his death on the Cross. He taught that God forgives the penitent and desires fellowship with men, but other prophets taught the same. Christ's present influence is like that of many great men who have lived. It is mediated to us through the Gospels, especially the Sermon on the Mount and related ethical teachings. The New Testament records themselves are conglomerates of a little truth and a great deal of fiction drawn from the surrounding ethnic religions or the imagination of the writers themselves.[5]

Against such modern "infidelity," the militant fundamentalist movement arose.

AN HISTORICAL SKETCH

Fundamentalism is composed of several elements: the revivalistic pietism of frontier America, the millenarian fervor of the nineteenth century, the strict confessional theology of the "Old Princeton School," the Bible conference and Bible institute movements which arose with evangelist Dwight L. Moody, along with a strong stream of reactionary sociopolitical movements. In this sense it is typical of American religion, which has seldom manifested that harmonious integration of intellect, emotion and will which is said to be the mark of the well-adjusted individual. In every period in our history there has been tension between religious movements which emphasized *rational thought,* movements which stressed *feelings,* and movements which encouraged *direct action.*

The stern theocracy of Puritan New England was a product of the lengthy doctrinal preaching of its ministers. Religion was orthodox doctrine—and woe to the man whose views were incorrect. For Church and State were one. Heresy was punished not only because it threatened men's souls, but also because it weakened the authority of secular government. The refusal to believe was too dangerous to social order to be permitted. A heretic was a man with ideas too subversive to be tolerated. On one side stood the traditionalists secure in the doctrine of an absolute God who determined the salvation or damnation of each man before his birth. Such a God was easily kept at arm's length during the course of one's day-to-day life. On the other side was the liberal intellectualism of Charles Chauncy of Boston with its God of benevolence, its discouragement of unrestricted emotionalism in religious services, and its confidence in human reason. But between these two ideological interpretations of religion stood the itinerant revivalists who reproved men for their sins, threatened them with hell, and called them to conversion at hectic meetings punctuated by the shrieking, trembling, and fainting of the repentant. And while traditionalists, liberals, and revivalists argued the need for personal regeneration, other Christians discussed questions of social order and government which would find violent resolution forty years later in the American War of Independence.

The Great Awakening was really a series of revivals which exploded like firecrackers between 1734 and 1750. The movement began in 1734 with the preaching of Jonathan Edwards at Northampton, Mass. Edwards delivered a series of sermons which emphasized the wrath and anger of God. He carried his hearers "to the very pit of hell," striking them with terror, causing them to cry out in fear. Hundreds were converted and experienced the forgiving grace of God. Tales of the emotion-filled meetings spread throughout the colonies. Soon the Presbyterian minister, William Tennent, Sr., was training revivalistic preachers in Neshaminy, Penna. In 1739 George Whitefield, a close friend of the Wesleys, arrived in the colonies to conduct public meetings and bind the various local revivals into one great movement. As H. Richard Niebuhr observed, America "cannot eradicate, if it would, the marks left upon its social memory, upon its institutions and habits, by an awakening of God that was simultaneous with its awakening to national self-consciousness." [6]

Pietistic individualism was firmly rooted in American religion during the early years of the republic. Direct access to God without the need for "externals"—priests, sacraments, liturgy, church organizations—suited the temperament of the rugged, self-sufficient individualists of the American frontier. As sociologist Bryan Wilson notes:

> Salvation by individual decision to accept Christ fitted circumstances in which men had to decide things for themselves, without the strong social pressures of a settled social order. . . . Revivalism was suited to the atomised character of frontier society, and was one of the few agencies that could bring men together . . .[7]

An important development during the frontier period was the spread of millennialism. At the beginning of the nineteenth century, revivalistic Protestantism looked forward to the gradual permeation of American society and its structures by the gospel message. But disappointed expectations and a general worsening in economic conditions gave birth to the socially pessimistic premillennialism of later fundamentalism, *i.e.* the conviction that no substantial improvement in the human condition is possible before the second coming of Jesus.[8] The simple people of the frontier, impatient with the unsatisfactory conditions of their daily lives, flocked to such leaders as William Miller and Joseph Smith (founders of the Adventist Church and the Church of Jesus Christ of the Latter-Day Saints, respectively) who proclaimed the impending end of the age and the coming of a divine utopia. Miller made the unfortunate mistake of predicting a definite date for the second advent; and Smith was murdered by a mob in

Carthage, Ill. But the sense of dissatisfaction with the present world and the expectation of a better age which may dawn at any moment have never faded from American religion. As we shall see, the doctrine of the imminent return of Jesus has always been a central fundamentalist conviction.

But could frontier individualism cope with the complexities of modern life? Could the momentary excitement of a camp-meeting conversion enable a man to deal with the rising price of manufactured goods, the collapse of farm produce prices, the problems of urban life, class struggle, labor disputes, riots, strikes, sweatshops, and alcoholism? For such were the problems of America in the 1870's and '80's as immigration, industrialization, and urbanization transformed the character of our national existence.

What was the response of the churches? According to William Bos and Clyde Faries:

> Most preachers ignored the gathering storm. . . . They urged people to be saved, explained doctrine, pictured the glories of heaven, and warned of the torments of hell, but did not mention the crises that tore at the soul of the country.[9]

If everyone were to accept Christ, these preachers contended, there would be no need for social reform. But more and more American Christianity recognized the need to confront the economic and social issues of the day.

Those who preached to the uneducated and poor continued to offer salvation as an escape from the cruelties of everyday existence. Dwight L. Moody, the greatest evangelist of the nineteenth century, could still proclaim to huge assemblages: "Accept of Jesus Christ personally; take Him in your heart now; let go of your own self; cease all your efforts, and just lay hold of Him. . . . Believe . . . Just simply believe." [10] But how different was the new "Social Gospel" with its insistence that the true Christian life was unselfish dedication to the improvement of society and its institutions.

The Social Gospel movement was strongly influenced by Darwin's theory of evolution. The Bible was no longer regarded as a collection of infallible texts providing authoritative guidance for all matters of faith and life. Instead the new biblical criticism treated the Scriptures as a record of an ongoing religious development, a collection of ancient writings which were better interpreted in light of the discoveries of archaeology, linguistics, and textual criticism than by an intuitive, devotional approach. The Bible was considered a record of man's progressive understanding of God, not an inspired, inerrant revelation of an immutable deity.

The peace, prosperity, and technological progress of the early twentieth century seemed to confirm the Darwinism of the Christian liberals. Mankind *was* making perceptible progress. Little by little the world *was* getting better and nothing could arrest its upward course. To be sure, there were those who rejected the rosy expectations of the modernists. In 1895 a Bible conference at Niagara Falls had drawn up a statement of "fundamental" truths which separated "true" Christians from "modern apostates." These essential doctrines were: 1) the virgin birth of Jesus, 2) Christ's death on the cross as payment for man's sins, 3) Christ's bodily resurrection, 4) the actual, bodily return of Jesus to earth to establish the earthly kingdom of God, and 5) the absolute inerrancy of the Bible.

In 1909 two wealthy Californians, Lyman and Milton Stewart underwrote the publication and distribution of the *Fundamentals,* a series of twelve volumes which defended the five essential truths of the Niagara Falls conference and which attacked the position of the modernists. Henceforth the term "fundamentalist" would refer to those who combined the emotionalism of the revivalists with uncompromising dedication to the "fundamentals." And American Christianity would be split into two warring camps.

Even before the fundamentalist-modernist controversy, the seeds of the destruction of liberalism were being sown. Especially in Europe, liberal optimism was dealt a vicious blow by the horrors of World War I. Mankind had not been making irreversible progress toward a golden age of peace, prosperity and unselfish benevolence after all. Sin was something more than the primitive urges which man had overcome in his unbroken, upward evolution. In America, however, faith in the perfectability of man and his social institutions would survive even the Depression and another world war. And Reinhold Niebuhr would come to fame by pricking the bubble of optimism in liberal religion. The world would change so rapidly that only change itself could be regarded as permanent. By the 1960's the liberal faith would appear as obsolete and as foolish as the fundamentalist attack on evolutionary modernism had seemed to H. L. Mencken in the twenties. Nevertheless, the fundamentalist attack upon the modernists and the liberals' counterattack upon the conservatives would persist.

After the First World War

Before the First World War, the fundamentalists were haphazardly organized and poorly led. Their various small societies were of little influence. But after the war new leaders emerged in every part of the country—Frank J. Norris from Texas, Gerald Winrod from Kansas, Harry Rimmer from Los Angeles. In 1919 the first national convention of fundamentalists was held at Moody Bible Institute in Chicago, and the World's Christian Fundamentalist Association (WCFA) was formed for the purpose of purging modernistic elements from schools, seminaries, and local churches. In 1924 William Jennings Bryan, former Secretary of State and thrice Democratic presidential candidate, appeared at the WCFA convention in Minneapolis. At last, fundamentalism had a nationally famous and popular leader.

The year 1925 was climactic for American fundamentalism. John T. Scopes, a Tennesse schoolteacher, had been arrested and charged with violating a Tennessee statute which prohibited the teaching of evolution in public schools. Although Scopes was found guilty, his defense by doughty civil libertarian Clarence Darrow and the newspaper coverage of sharp-tongued H. L. Mencken turned public sympathy against the fundamentalists.[11] Also, the death of Bryan within days of the conclusion of the trial left the movement without a leader. Interest in fundamentalism drained away, attendance at their annual conventions declined sharply, the old ardor disappeared. At the 1930 convention of the WCFA, not one of the scheduled speeches even mentioned modernism or evolution.

The tide had turned. Before the Scopes trial the fundamentalists in the major Protestant denominations had caused the dismissal or resignation of a number of modernists. Shortly before the Scopes trial, Harry Emerson Fosdick abandoned the pulpit of the First Presbyterian Church of New York City rather than submit to the jurisdiction and authority of the Presbyterian Church (U.S.A.). But in 1929 the conservative forces of J. Gresham Machen suffered defeat before the General Assembly of the same denomination when they attempted to prevent the infiltration of the faculty of Princeton Theological Seminary by liberals. The separatist course had been set. No longer would the fundamentalists force the modernists to leave the major Protestant denominations. Now the conservative forces would separate themselves from the "apostate" parent bodies, and create their own orthodox seminaries, mission boards, local congregations, vacation resorts, periodicals, radio stations, and denominational structures. To be sure, not all fundamentalists would leave the major denominations—fundamentalist camps exist within the United Presbyterian Church, U.S.A. to this very day. Furthermore, the scarcity of "modernists" in the Southern Baptist Convention and among the Missouri Lutherans spared them the struggles between fundamentalists and liberals. But other denominations were forever disrupted. The American Baptist Convention (formerly known as the "Northern Baptists"), to cite but one example, has never recovered from schisms occasioned by the fundamentalist-modernist controversy.[12]

Ecclesiastical power had shifted from the fundamentalists to their opponents. But more harmful to the fundamentalist cause was a general change of attitudes. As Allan H. Sager remarks, "Fundamentalists were not defeated; the climate changed and they found themselves no longer a viable force on the American theological scene." [13] For the authoritarian faith of the fundamentalists ran counter to basic assumptions of twentieth-century culture: the confidence in the power of human reason, science, and technology to solve all human problems; the belief that man should be free to solve his problems untrammelled by government or religious restrictions; the unwillingness of free men to allow traditional norms and conventions to interfere with the pursuit of pleasure. The widespread hedonism of America in the twenties was immune to fundamentalist preachments. Increasingly, fundamentalism became the voice of rural America; while the progressivistic, scientistic, and socially involved faith of the modernists was pressed into service by modern urban society to sanctify the American Way.

The fundamentalists resisted a trend which deserved to be resisted: the tendency to confuse religious tradition with the spirit of the age. In the words of one conservative theologian, they "sought to prove that modernism and Biblical Christianity were incompatible. In this way the fundamentalist movement preserved the faith once for all delivered to the saints." [14] But by attacking the wrong targets—evolution and biblical criticism instead of the unprincipled pursuit of wealth and pleasure—the fundamentalists doomed themselves to the fringes of American religious and social life.

Yet even liberal theologian L. Harold DeWolf praises the fundamentalists for their significant contributions to the life of the Church. He declares:

> The fundamentalists continued a stress on Bible study and on the biblical message through times when the Bible was being widely neglected. . . . Insistence by the fundamentalists upon clarity and directness of theological affirmation was needed as it is still needed. . . . The fundamentalists have stressed man's imperative need of God. . . . They have maintained the doctrine of a personal God, a Father with whom we can com-

municate in prayer, a Father purposively concerned with our human need. . . . Also, they have focused attention on the person and work of Christ, and the urgency of personal decision for Christ. . . . Finally, the fundamentalists have cultivated among millions of Americans the practical piety of earnest personal prayer, world-wide evangelistic concern, generous giving, and warm Christian fellowship.[15]

FUNDAMENTALISM: PHENOMENOLOGICAL DESCRIPTION

First and foremost, fundamentalism is a religion of personal salvation. It is conversion *experience* which is essential, not doctrine. According to fundamentalists, God has a simple plan of salvation. Just as the universe is governed by physical laws which have been discovered by science, so is man's relationship to God governed by spiritual laws which are found in the Bible.

The root of all human problems is the perversity of the human heart. Nothing short of miraculous spiritual regeneration can change man; and unless man is transformed he can scarcely hope to solve any of the trying problems of his personal or social existence. The editors of the neo-evangelical journal *Christianity Today* counsel Christians to "endeavor to rear a superstructure of social justice and righteousness," but remind their readers that "nothing short of supernatural faith in Jesus provides an effectual remedy for the disease of sin." [16]

Writing at the beginning of the present century, William James reported:

> To be converted, to be regenerated, to receive grace, to experience religion, to gain an assurance, are so many phrases which denote the process, gradual or sudden, by which a self hitherto divided, and consciously wrong, inferior, and unhappy, becomes unified and consciously right, superior, and happy, in consequence of its firmer hold upon religious realities. This at least is what conversion signifies in general terms, whether or not we believe that a direct divine operation is needed to bring such a moral change about.[17]

Dynamics of Crisis Conversion

Crisis conversion—the sudden, emotion-charged passage from one plane of existence to another—is viewed by many psychologists as a normal adolescent phenomenon (although it is by no means limited to adolescents). As the teenager stands on the brink of adulthood, he becomes painfully aware of his incompleteness and imperfection. In consequence, he broods, becomes morbidly introspective, is attacked by depression and anxiety, and feels sinful and guilty—as if he had transgressed some unknown moral law. A hundred new urges disturb him. A multitude of new voices demand his attention. A thousand possibilities present themselves to him, leaving him confused and bewildered.

The adolescent struggles after a sense of identity, agonizes after a hopeful direction for his future. He is on his own—neither his elders nor his peers can solve his dilemma for him. With every passing year, the pressures mount, the need to choose becomes more unavoidable, the present appears more terrifying. Considering the paucity of emotional support the young receive from their elders (who both envy and despise them) and the temptations to which they are exposed (drugs, sexual permissiveness, the boredom-spurred violence of the campus and the ghetto), it is a wonder that so many survive with reasonably whole skins or psyches and find a place for themselves in adult life.

There is in all of us a hunger for something absolute, for something worthy of our unconditional devotion, for something in which we can believe and which, in turn, will transform our lives. For all of us are discontented with ourselves: tired of our failures, dissatisfied with our limitations, sick unto death of our weaknesses. Most of us have learned to live with ourselves, to excuse our transgressions, to accept our foibles. But the young find all possibilities limitless, all decisions matters of life or death. And when the strain becomes too great, the self-dissatisfied young person does not try to make peace with himself, but rather he seeks to escape from himself. He finds a better or ideal state of existence. He falls in love. Or he finds a movement to which he can sacrifice himself. Or he is born again.

Religious conversion, romantic love, and enthusiasm for a cause are identical in this respect—they offer an opportunity for the individual to lose his limited self through union with a greater reality. The ardor of the religious convert, the dedication of the zealot, and the rapture of the lover release a flood of feelings which sweep away doubts and despair. As psychologist Theodor Reik observed: "An irresistible power from within seems to govern and lead the recipient, floating through him and carrying him beyond himself." [18]

Revivalistic conversion is only one such response. During the past few years we have met converts who were every bit as zealous on behalf of drug-induced mysticism, astrology, or Krishna Consciousness as fundamentalists are on behalf of Christ. The pattern is always the same: *a*) radical self-dissatisfaction grows into a sense of cosmic discontent; *b*) the socially acceptable solutions to one's personal dilemmas fail to work; *c*) solutions which are condemned by society as a whole but advocated by one's fellow malcontents prove even more worthless than the socially accepted answers; *d*) a mood of quiet despair prevails; *e*) suddenly through a flash of insight everything falls in place—the malcontent finds the answer and his life is transformed.

Conversion experience is paramount; and theological explanation is only secondary. But note the amount of doctrine which is implicit in the salvation experience. For the intention of this powerful affective state is: *a*) acceptance of Jesus Christ as personal savior and Lord; *b*) acceptance of the authority of the Bible as the Word of God; *c*) acceptance of the legitimacy of "religious authority" as represented by the preacher, evangelist, gospel tract publisher, etc., to mediate the presence of God as felt in the salvation experience; *d*) acceptance of a harsh, pessimistic view of one's own nature and of human nature in general; and *e*) renunciation of the control of one's life to the lordship of God as mediated by intense personal feelings, the Bible, the Church, religious leaders, etc. All these and more are implicit in the conversion experience itself; and once conversion has occurred the consequences begin flowering like so many previously planted seeds.

MAJOR DOCTRINES OF FUNDAMENTALISM

We will now consider briefly each of the doctrines implicit in the fundamentalist conversion experience.

Jesus Christ as Personal Savior and Lord

At the beginning, acceptance of Christ means only the recognition of the human dilemma as described by the revivalist, and a personal resolve to accept the conversion experience. Often this inner experience is accompanied by the recitation of a prayer of contrition. The moment of conversion is typically characterized by a profound sense of relief or release, and a sense of inner warmth and security (interpreted by fundamentalists as the indwelling presence of the Holy Spirit or the presence of the divine Christ). The acceptance of Jesus Christ as Lord means that after conversion the individual seeks to live in accordance with the will of Christ as revealed in the Scriptures and through an inner sense of assurance which accompanies certain acts, thoughts, plans for the future, etc., but which is absent from others. Consciously or unconsciously, the convert attempts to preserve the powerful and distinctive affective tone by which he was overcome during the conversion experience, and to achieve this same inner state in all subsequent experiences.

The Bible as the Word of God

Since the proclamation of biblical texts was the source of the conversion experience, it is natural for the convert to regard this book as unique and authoritative. For either the book and the convert's experience are true or both are false. The intensity of the convert's personal transformation will allow for no other possibilities. Guided by revivalistic teachers and preachers, the convert comes to regard the Bible as a divinely inspired, error-free, comprehensive, and unambiguous message from God to man. Although there are many theories of inspiration held by conservative theologians, the very essence of fundamentalism is the claim that the original documents of the Scriptures were inerrantly dictated by God to men and that everything contained in them is infallible. To many fundamentalists, this means that the Bible is the final authority in all matters—history, geography, chronology, biology, zoology, geology, physics as well as matters of faith and conscience. It is not unusual to meet fundamentalists who believe that the only education men need is biblical education, and that modern colleges and universities are satanic entrapments which destroy the faith of Christian young people with the "lies" of modern science.

The convert is told that it is his duty to read the Bible regularly, and therein to seek guidance for his life. Fundamentalists believe that God speaks to believers through the Scriptures, revealing his will for their lives by granting them a sense of assurance and comfort or striking them with feelings of conviction and discomfort as they read the Bible. Fundamentalists also seek to classify the contents of the Scriptures according to topics (salvation, prophecy, Christian life, the Holy Spirit, etc.) through the use of concordances (books which list all the passages in the Bible mentioning a given word, *e.g.* "love"), chain reference Bibles (marginal notes indicate other passages on given topics), topical text books (much like concordances, but arranged according to general subjects instead of single words). Almost without exceptions fundamentalists study the Bible "devotionally" (for personal comfort and guidance) rather than historically. Fundamentalists have little sense of the Bible as a collection of documents written over the course of many centuries which reflect the religious development of the Hebrew nation and the early church. The Scriptures, they contend, were not given to be *appreciated* through historico-grammatical exegesis, but to be *obeyed* as God's message to the individual reader. At times, the Bible degenerates into a divine punchboard filled with magic answers. Instead of carefully considering the possible alternatives available to him in a given situation, the believer merely throws open his Bible and immediately finds "God's will" in the first verse which strikes his eye.

The Legitimacy of "Religious Authorities"

Since fundamentalism is more concerned with sincere feelings than clearly articulated theology or orderly ecclesiastical polity, it often produces a restlessness of spirit which borders on anarchy. Rapidly recruited converts, whose religious knowledge is limited to a few intense hours of experience, are loath to settle down in the established congregations of traditional denominations. They distrust traditional creeds, formalized worship, theological discussion, or anything which might distract Christians from their major responsibility—the conversion of sinners.

Converts tend to associate themselves with the group headed by the revivalist through whom they were converted. This is the most frequent pattern, and provides the convert with the greatest sense of continuity. But what of the converts of itinerant tent evangelists or such notable "interdenominational" preachers as Billy Graham? Obviously the evangelistic organization cannot look after its converts; nor can it recommend churches to them if it is to maintain the impartiality which it owes to the many different churches that sponsor its mass meetings. Again, the convictions implicit in the conversion experience tend to guide the convert to a local congregation supportive of the convert's experience. Conversely, the convert will not stay long in a congregation which provides an adverse setting for the preservation of the convert's new inner state.

Eventually, the convert finds a local congregation which

supports and encourages his new world view. But a basic weakness has always afflicted revivalism. Its notion of church is basically negative or cultic. Since it is easier to recognize and condemn the errors of established churches than to establish positive alternatives, the fundamentalist has found it simpler to attack his enemies—real or imagined—than to deal creatively with society and its problems. The extreme emphasis upon individual experience promotes the notorious schismatic tendency of fundamentalism. Some fundamentalist leaders and diminishing numbers of followers have withdrawn from subgroup after subgroup in order to protect their own purity from the ever more subtle deviations from "the truth of God's Word." The highly individualized, emotional, and anti-intellectual approach to religion advocated by the fundamentalists has enormously influenced the character of American religion. Again and again, throughout our national history, revivalism has reinvigorated established churches, led to the creation of Sunday schools, home and foreign mission societies, as well as colleges and seminaries for the training of Christian ministers. But it also introduced a spirit of dissension which has constantly divided the Church.

A Pessimistic View of Human Nature

Not only does the fundamentalist believe that man is by nature a rebel against the will of God, but also that the depravity of the individual dooms all human undertakings to failure. An Evangelical Covenant pastor in Berkeley, Calif., recently castigated the involvement of fellow clergymen in the peace movement and civil rights agitation. "Why can't they realize," he publicly elocuted, "that war is only a symptom? that racial discrimination is only a symptom? The real problem is *sin*." [19]

Human nature is perverse and irremediable. The world is destined to become worse and worse until the coming of Christ. As Hal Lindsey preaches: "When the Lord returns, there will be no war, there will be no racial strife, there will be no poverty or hunger, there will be no air pollution. Jesus is really gonna get it together." [20] The impending doom of the world is seen as an occasion for rejoicing. "Maranatha! The Lord is coming!"

Emphasis on the imminence of Christ's return has always produced paradoxical repercussions. Some Christians are inspired by this doctrine to an earnest dedication of their lives to the Christian gospel. After all, "Only one life, 'twill soon be past. Only what's done for Christ will last." But others use the impending end of the age as an excuse to "cop out," to abandon responsibilities and discipline. Earlier in this century, observes Allan H. Sager:

> Many fundamentalists declared that indeed a glorious future was sure to come, but that it would come through the arbitrary stroke of God, not through the struggles of men to realize illusive social ideals. They shared the belief that the world was essentially evil and that not only would it remain so but would grow more so until God himself finally destroyed it. Indeed, the logic of this position pushed to the conclusion that the worse the world got, the more reason for hope in the imminent Second Coming.[21]

Thus, the church is seen not as an agency for the amelioration of human misery but as an ark through which a select number of righteous souls can be saved from the impending cataclysm. The world is lost. Prepare to leave. Such is the fundamentalist message.

Renunciation of Control of One's Life

The notions of the depravity of man and the futility of all human effort hardly elicit self-confidence or self-assertion in the young convert. After all, where did his freedom get him in the past? If he had not experienced an intense sense of failure and self-dissatisfaction, conversion would never have occurred in the first place. The convert places his life in the hands of a higher authority. In psychological terms, this means that ego-control is surrendered to the demands of the super-ego. The enhanced affective tone resulting from the conversion experience filters into the area of compulsions and inhibitions. Inner demands, directions, and prohibitions are more vivid than ever.

The convert adopts a way of life structured according to the specific dos and don'ts of the religious group which he has joined. Regardless of specific sectarian differences, all fundamentalist groups advocate regular Bible reading and prayer, attendance at church services, participation in the sacraments or ordinances of baptism and the Lord's Supper, financial contributions to the support of one's local congregation, avoidance of worldliness (prohibited by most groups as "worldly" are gambling, social dancing, attendance at movies or the theater, smoking, sexual contact outside of marriage, etc.), and, *above all, the winning of others.*

The essential negativity of fundamentalism is most apparent in its understanding of morality. A good man is one who *refrains from* behavior such as smoking, drinking, social dancing, and card playing; a good woman refrains from using cosmetics, jewelry, and immodest dress. As long as a man or woman *avoids* these temptations, he or she is considered righteous in the eyes of the community of born-again Christians. The result is a negative or cultic ethic more concerned with status in the religious in-group than responsibilities to one's neighbor. The revivalistic Christian has been so concerned with shunning trivial social practices that he has been generally unconcerned with major social issues.

FUNDAMENTALISM AS A RELIGIOUS MOVEMENT: THE SECTARIAN RESPONSE

The internal logic of fundamentalism is more compatible with the *sect* rather than the *church* pattern of response to the world. A church is reconciled with secular culture. A sect rejects it. Membership in a church is usually determined by birth. But a sect is "a voluntary society, composed of strict and definite Christian believers bound to each other by the fact that all have experienced 'the new birth.' "[22] Membership in a church confers prestige in the eyes of the local secular community. Membership in a sect indicates the individual's rejection of society and often leads to his rejection by society.

Churches tend to be tolerant of the claims of other religious groups. As a result, they seldom engage in proselytizing efforts. Sects, on the other hand, view all other religious bodies with hostility. A sect is an elite. As Bryan Wilson notes:

> The sect, as the sole possessor of true doctrine, of appropriate ritual and of warranted standards of rectitude in social behavior, regards itself as a people set apart, making claim, if not always to absolutely exclusive salvation, at least to the fullest blessings.[23]

The tolerance shown by churches extends to the behavior of their members. Seldom is an individual chastened for immoral acts or heretical opinions. But sects expel the unworthy, the careless, the insufficiently committed, and the misguided. Churches allow their members to regard religion as one of several responsibilities of more or less equal importance. But sects demand that dedication to the religious group take precedence over all other allegiances (family, recreation, community affairs, politics, etc.). Churches provide individuals with the emotional encouragement and consolation which they require in order to be productive members of society at large. Sects provide exclusivistic fellowships through which individuals may resist the demands of society. The conservative denominations of today are the sects of yesterday that have made their peace with secular society. As sociologists of religion have demonstrated, ". . . if the sect is defined rigorously, it cannot last beyond the founding generation. Family life, increasing wealth and respectability, and routinization [the development of organization, structure, and standards for the training and selection of leaders], with the passage of time lead to accommodation by the sect."[24] Thus most sects have become churches within forty years of their inception. Originally a movement of protest against modernism, fundamentalism has become more an attitude of dogmatic intolerance and intractable resistance to denominational Christianity. According to Carnell, "fundamentalism made one capital mistake. This is why it converted from a religious movement to a religious mentality. Unlike the Continental Reformers and the English dissenters, the fundamentalists failed to develop an affirmative world view." [25] As a highly ideological mentality, fundamentalism is, in Carnell's view, "intransigent and inflexible; it expects conformity; it fears academic liberty. . . . It has cut itself off from the general stream of culture, philosophy, and ecclesiastical tradition." [26] The revivalistic heritage has done much to promote religion in America, but it has also made the Christian faith "a stranger to large segments of American intellectual, cultural, and political life." [27]

FUNDAMENTALISM SINCE WORLD WAR II

Since the Second World War fundamentalism has moved in three directions: *1*) anti-Communism; *2*) neo-evangelicalism; and *3*) mass evangelism. Each movement is a response to the over-all decline in fundamentalist influence upon American life. As Dale G. Leathers reports:

> For almost three decades before 1960, fundamentalist values and the political positions for which these values provide sanctions were quite unsalable.[28]

As we have seen, fundamentalist energies had been devoted to combating modernism. But the decline of liberal confidence in the inevitable progress of mankind, and, paradoxically, the triumph of liberal social concerns (for example, the New Deal attempt to guarantee the financial security of the poor, the elderly, and the unemployed) left fundamentalism without an enemy to fight.

Christian Anti-Communism

By the 1950's the conservative religious cause was approaching desperation. The answer for many fundamentalists, including evangelists Billy James Hargis and Carl McIntire, was the development of the issue of anti-Communism. According to these "Christian anti-Communists," there is a worldwide Communist conspiracy to take control of the governments and social institutions of every nation. In the United States, the Communist technique is internal subversion, the gradual infiltration of government (local, state, and federal), the communications media, and even the churches. In theory, Christian anti-Communism is dedicated to informing the public of the threat to democracy. In fact, it lends religious coloration to reactionary politics, branding as "Communist" all programs with which it disagrees (*e.g.*, civil rights, the peace movement, campus radicalism). By wrapping himself in the American flag, the Christian anti-Communist identifies the Gospel with a given political stance just as earlier fundamentalists defined themselves in relation to a philosophical-scientific issue (evolution). From its inception the Christian anti-Communist movement has tended to identify the will of God with America and the activities of the devil with "godless, atheistic" communism. It sees all Communists—the Soviet bloc as well as Red China, Marxist humanists together with strict Stalinists, American Trotskyites as well as Cuban Socialists—as one vast, monolithic threat to "God-fearing, freedom-loving" America. Futhermore, the Christian anti-Communists attack individuals and groups which are critical of America's national life or international policy, branding them as pro-Communist and anti-Christian. As a result of the efforts of the self-proclaimed "defenders of liberty" there has been, notes Jerald C. Brauer, "constant pressure from within and without the Churches to eulogize everything in American life and to decry all criticism of existing society." [29]

According to the "premillennialist" interpretation of the Bible which is shared by the majority of fundamentalists, we are living in the last days. ("Society has been morally deteriorating since the days of Adam and the downward trend must continue until Christ comes to set things right by a cosmic catastrophe.") Moral and social ills—wars, famines, earthquakes, political corruption, etc.—are signs of the impending end of the present evil age. When the situation reaches the pinnacle of wickedness, Jesus will descend from heaven, and the true company of the righteous then alive as well as the resurrected saints of former times will rise to meet him in the air. There Christ and his church will abide for seven years. With this removal or "rapture" of the righteous from the world, a period of tribulation shall descend upon mankind; strange and fearsome events shall occur. The Jews will return to their national homeland. The Antichrist will appear, establish his capital at Babylon, and demand the allegiance of all men. His forces shall ravage the earth. Refusing to acknowledge his sovereignty, the Jews will feel the full weight of his wrath. In their darkest hour, as they are surrounded by the hordes of the Antichrist, they shall be miraculously rescued. Jesus will descend upon the Mount of Olives with his heavenly company and rout the forces of the Antichrist in the climactic battle of Armageddon. The Jews will accept Jesus as their messiah and lord, and he will reign for a thousand years from his temporal throne in Jerusalem.[30]

At the end of the "millennium" Satan will be released from the pit and war against Christ and his saints. In the final battle Satan and his cohorts will be defeated. Satan will be condemned forever to torment, the ungodly dead will be resurrected "unto judgment" and consigned to the eternal flames. The universe will perish by fire as Jesus and the redeemed ascend to the eternal bliss of heaven.[31]

Although not all fundamentalists will accept every detail of this prophetic scheme, they are in essential agreement on the general outline: the history of mankind is the chronicle of man's apostasy; the world is doomed to its unfathomable and irremediable perversity; only the intervention of God can save the world from destruction; ultimately the present world must perish and a new order take its place. The belief that Jesus could return at any moment has characterized revivalistic Christianity for over a hundred years. But no leader has been surer that the events of his day were the final, catastrophic falling away from God than has ultrafundamentalist Carl McIntire.

President of the first-year class at Princeton Theological Seminary, McIntire followed his mentor, J. Gresham Machen, and his conservative party to Westminster Theological Seminary in 1929. It was already clear to McIntire that the forces of apostasy were in control of the major Protestant denominations, their mission boards, and their schools. In addition, the forces of Satan were behind the international Communist conspiracy which was infiltrating American life in numerous guises. According to McIntire, Christians should flee from the apostate churches, and as a saving remnant dedicate their lives to resisting the Communist threat. Throughout his career, McIntire has attacked "modernism," the Federal Council of Churches (now the National Council of Churches), Communist influence, and "every system alien to the Bible." The political power structure of the United States, the social gospel liberalism of the mainline churches, the Civil Rights movement, the New Left, the local schools and churches throughout America are considered part and parcel of the dominion of Satan. Always eager to reprove other fundamentalists for being less "separated" from the modern apostasy than he and thus being the tools of Satan, in recent years McIntire has found his staunchest allies not among the fundamentalists but among the forces of the radical right. Now alienated even from the American Council of Christian Churches which he founded, McIntire is moving his power base from New Jersey to Florida where he is assured of the blessings of the most reactionary elements. (As of this writing, the financial support expected by McIntire in the Cape Kennedy area has failed to materialize.)

McIntire has supported and accepted the praise of Governors George Wallace and Lester Maddox, has steadfastly demanded American military victory in Viet Nam, has reproved America's national leaders for not having gone to war with the forces of "godless Communism," [32] has vilified the U.N., has opposed gun control legislation, has fought floridation and Medicare as not only socialistic but "totalitarian," and has defended the Minutemen. He is currently leading "victory marches" in various parts of the nation and conducting public protests against President Nixon's visit to the People's Republic of China.

McIntire's zeal for political causes had led him into a dangerous self-contradiction. According to his biblical eschatology, all the "evils" that he opposes—Social Security, the income tax, Medicare, a powerful Federal Government, welfare, Civil Rights, the peace movement, the liberalism of the churches, ecumenism, etc.—are "symptomatic of . . . the tyranny and collectivism of American life brought on by the internal conspiracy." [33] But should the causes which McIntire advocates triumph and the "evils" which he opposes be abolished, it would prove that the Bible was wrong. For the success of McIntire's program would mean, notes Erling Jorstad, that "the liberal conspiracy had been destroyed and God's elect had gained control of this planet *before* the Pretribulation Rapture and the Battle of Armageddon." [34] Hence, McIntire is left in the position of advocating "a program which if adopted would destroy his most cherished beliefs." [35]

Not only is Christian anti-communism politically repressive; it is theologically heterodox—as fundamentalists themselves are beginning to recognize. As heir to American revivalism, fundamentalism is intensely individualistic: "Unless a man be born again he cannot see the kingdom of God." Fundamentalism has always rejected the notion that a man is a Christian because he lives in a nominally Christian country, is the child of Christian parents, or belongs to a Christian church. Salvation is not a matter of location, nationality, race, birth, or religious affiliation; it is a matter of personal faith and conversion. Hence, the true fundamentalist regards America as "a pagan nation inhabited by a minority of committed Christians."[36] He will call his fellow Americans not to a holy war of "Christian America" against "godless Communism," but to repentance and spiritual rebirth. The fundamentalist knows that the inclusion of a few theistic formulas in the utterances of our politicians, upon our coins, or in the Pledge of Allegiance no more makes the United States a "Christian nation" than the wearing of belt buckles emblazoned "Gott mit uns" sanctified the purposes of Nazi soldiers.

The New Evangelicals

A second direction has been "neo-evangelicalism," an attempt on the part of sophisticated fundamentalists to modify the social isolationism and harsh dogmatism of classic fundamentalism. In the words of Harold Ockenga:

> The new evangelicalism embraces the full orthodoxy of fundamentalism, but manifests a social consciousness and responsibility which was strangely absent from fundamentalism. The new evangelicalism concerns itself not only with personal salvation, doctrinal truth and an eternal point of reference, but also with the problems of race, of war, of class struggle, of liquor control, of juvenile delinquency, of immorality, and of national imperialism. . . . The new evangelicalism believes that orthodox Christians cannot abdicate their responsibility in the social scene.[37]

The "new evangelicals" often reject the designation "fundamentalists." As J. Gresham Machen remarked a generation ago:

> The term fundamentalism is distasteful to the present writer and to many persons who hold views similar to his. It seems to suggest that we are adherents to some strange new sect, whereas in point of fact we are conscious simply of maintaining historic Christian faith and moving in the great central current of Christian life.[38]

Ockenga contends that although the doctrinal positions of fundamentalism and neo-evangelicalism are identical, the strategy of new evangelicals represents a definite advance upon the methods of the older conservatives. "Time revealed certain weaknesses in the fundamentalist cause," notes Ockenga. The fundamentalists were maneuvered into a defensive posture by the forces of ecclesiastical modernism. As a result, fundamentalism was reduced "to a holding tactic, impotent in denominational machinery and indifferent to societal problems rising in the secular world." [39]

The fundamentalists contributed to their own difficulties by adopting a heterodox ecclesiology, i.e. the erroneous doctrine that the Church consists only of believers who are orthodox in doctrine and separatist in ethics. According to Ockenga, "Emphasis was upon contention for the faith rather than missions, evangelism, education, and worship. The number of competent scholars declined in evangelical ranks as the decades passed." [40] By the mid-fifties, most publishers oriented toward the conservative Protestant market were issuing offset reproductions of orthodox classics from the past (the writings of Puritan divines, nineteenth-century Anglican Bible scholars, early twentieth-century guides to personal piety) to the virtual exclusion of works by contemporary evangelicals.

Rallying around the leadership of Billy Graham, the new evangelicals desire "to win a new respectability for orthodoxy in the academic circles by producing scholars who can defend the faith on intellectual ground," [41] to bring about the revival of orthodox Christianity in the midst of the secular world, to make the Christian faith the mainspring of needed social reforms, and to establish broad-based and permanent cooperation between all conservative Protestants. In pursuit of these goals, the new evangelical movement has founded several new seminaries, undertaken the publication of a major periodical, *Christianity Today,* and has begun to challenge "modernists" for control of the denominations from which the earlier fundamentalists have virtually fled. The new evangelicals advocate a strategy of infiltration. After all, Ockenga declares, modernists "have been using this strategy for years."

Unless a denomination has "officially and overtly repudiated biblical Christianity," he states, it should be infiltrated by evangelical Christians with the purpose of exerting an evangelical influence upon its programs and eventually gaining control of its institutions.[42]

The neo-evangelical condemns the fundamentalist disregard for the problems of society as irresponsible individualism. In an editorial concerning the 1964 Civil Rights Bill debate, *Christianity Today* reminded its readers:

> Patriotism demands individual concern in a matter so close to the public welfare. And patriotism is neither sub-Christian nor outmoded, even in this sophisticated age. For Christians it is plainly enjoined in Scripture. Moreover, ethics are united with patriotism; no Christian can stand passively by when the good of others is jeopardized. Obedience to the law of love for one's neighbor requires concern for the welfare of one's neighbor.[43]

But what principles are to guide the conscience of the Christian as he faces such a significant issue? The editors offered four guidelines:

> (1) The necessity for informed opinion. (2) The right of all Americans to equal rights of citizenship. (3) The obligation to respect those whose conscience leads them to convictions different from one's own. (4) The recognition that, essential as legislation is, moral problems are ultimately solved not by passing laws but by changing hearts.[44]

But if moral problems are "ultimately solved . . . by changing hearts," we may ask if Items 1, 2, and 3 are anything more than camouflage meant to give the impression that the evangelical Christian has developed a social conscience? For despite neo-evangelicalism's profession of commitment to "the problems of race, of war, of class struggle, . . . of immorality, and of national imperialism," there has appeared very little in the pages of *Christianity Today* during the fifteen years of its existence which would "disturb even the most conservative defenders of wealth and special privilege." We commend *Christianity Today* for having called attention to the pressing issues of the past decade and a half, for having informed conservative Protestants of national and international matters which they otherwise would have ignored, and for insisting that evangelical Christians take their citizenship as seriously as they take their religious convictions. But we wonder if their "hearts must be changed before problems can be solved" approach to the dilemmas of contemporary society is any more satisfactory than defensive separatism of the older fundamentalists. For neither the regressive ultrafundamentalists (McIntire, Hargis *et al.*) nor the sophisticated neo-evangelicals (Graham, Ockenga, Carl Henry, etc.) seem to realize that even if every man, woman, and child were to accept Christ, the task of solving America's social, political, moral, and ecological problems would only have begun.

Mass Evangelism

The third postwar direction taken by fundamentalism is represented by the mass evangelistic crusades of Billy Graham. In the twenty-three years following the 1949 Los Angeles Crusade which first brought him national attention, Graham has conducted public meetings throughout the United States, the United Kingdom, Europe, Asia, the Caribbean, Australia and New Zealand, Africa, the Middle East, and South America. His combined audiences are probably the largest in history to have heard a single speaker. Although he is not the first evangelist to have employed the techniques of the mass crusade with conspicuous success (consider the careers of Dwight L. Moody and Billy Sunday), he has added to the face-to-face meeting of expectant audience and charismatic preacher a whole new arsenal of evangelistic weapons, particularly an unexcelled utilization of the power of the mass media (press, radio, television, and film). His remarkable achievements as evangelist, his personal integrity and durability under the pressures of more than two decades of public scrutiny, and his association with successive American Presidents have won for him a respect and admiration which no previous evangelist has enjoyed. In addition, the popularity of the man has given prestige to a conservative Protestant message which for generations had been relegated by all observers to the fringes of American life.

Of nearly equal significance are the various youth-oriented evangelistic organizations including Youth for Christ (co-founded by Graham), Campus Crusade for Christ, and Inter-Varsity Christian Fellowship which have sprung up in the past quarter century. Dogmatically fundamentalistic and thoroughly revivalistic, these movements spread like wildfire in the late forties and early fifties, waned in the late fifties and during the sixties, and have shown a renewed vigor in recent months, particularly among the so-called Jesus People or Jesus Freaks. Based in California, these not-so-legitimate offspring of the street scene (drug addicts, hippies, runaways, drop-outs, members of motorcycle gangs, and Oriental cultists) and the perennial pietism of American Christendom, the Jesus Movement is on the march. Indeed, it is difficult to decide whether the evangelistic groups are responsible for the Jesus Movement or the Jesus Movement is responsible for the resurrection of the evangelistic groups! [45]

The continuing success of the Graham mass crusades in terms of attendance, inquirers, financial support, and the active participation of community and church leadership as well as the current revival of fundamentalism among the young suggest that the age of mass evangelism is far from over. In the words of George M. Wilson, Executive Vice President of the Billy Graham Evangelistic Association:

> Newsmen and others forecast the death of the crusades years ago. Many lay people and clergy alike claimed the conversions wouldn't last. Even Mr. Graham felt his ministry could dwindle after a few years. God saw differently.[46]

NOTES

1. Billy Graham, "Biblical Authority in Evangelism," *Christianity Today,* October 15, 1956, included in *A Christianity Today Reader,* p. 21.
2. Graham in *20 Years Under God: A Pictorial Review of the Billy Graham Ministries,* edited by George M. Wilson (Minneapolis, Minn.: World Wide Publications, 1970), pp. 152–153.
3. *The Case for Orthodox Theology* (Philadelphia: The Westminster Press, 1959), p. 113.
4. Shailer Mathews, *The Faith of Modernism* (New York: The Macmillan Company, 1924), pp. 22–36. See also his work, *The Growth of the Idea of God* (New York: The Macmillan Company, 1931).
5. Included in *Controversy in the Twenties: Fundamentalism, Modernism, and Evolution,* edited by Willard B. Gatewood, Jr. (Nashville: Vanderbilt University Press, 1969), pp. 381–382.
6. *The Kingdom of God in America* (Chicago: Willett, Clark and Company, 1937), p. 126.
7. *Religious Sects* (New York: McGraw-Hill Book Company, World University Library, 1970), p. 49.
8. Whitney R. Cross, *The Burnt-over District: The Social and Intellectual History of Enthusiastic Religion in Western New York 1800–1825* (Ithaca, N.Y.: Cornell University Press, 1956).
9. *Sermons in American History,* edited by DeWitte Holland (Nashville: Abingdon Press, 1971), p. 284.
10. "Evening Sermon," *Sermons in American History,* pp. 287–288.
11. See Raymond Ginger, *Six Days or Forever?* (Boston: Beacon Press, 1958).
12. For an account of the impact of the fundamentalist-modernist controversy upon the Baptists, Presbyterians, Methodists, Episcopalians, and Disciples of Christ, see Norman F. Furniss, *The Fundamentalist Controversy, 1918–1931* (Hamden, Conn.: Archon Books, 1963). For the history of the interaction of the fundamentalists and the Lutheran Church–Missouri Synod, see Milton L. Rudnick, *Fundamentalism & the Missouri Synod* (St. Louis: Concordia Publishing House, 1966).

    An excellent sourcebook of readings on the fundamentalist attack on evolution is provided by *Controversy in the Twenties: Fundamentalism, Modernism, and Evolution.* The sources of fundamentalist doctrine, particularly dispensational premillennialism, are documented in two important works by Ernest R. Sandeen: *The Origins of Fundamentalism, Toward a Historical Interpretation* (Philadelphia: Fortress Press, 1968) and *The Roots of Fundamentalism: British and American Millenarianism,* 1800–1930 (Chicago: University of Chicago Press, 1970).
13. "The Fundamentalist-Modernist Controversy, 1918–1930," *Preaching in American History,* edited by DeWitte Holland (Nashville: Abingdon Press, 1969), p. 270.
14. *The Case for Orthodox Theology, op. cit.,* p. 113.
15. *Present Trends in Christian Thought, op. cit.,* pp. 47–50.
16. Editorial, March 4, 1957.

17. *The Varieties of Religious Experience* (New York: Mentor Books, 1958), p. 157.
18. *Of Love and Lust,* (New York: Bantam Books, 1967) pp. 130–131.
19. At a "Bible Rap" sponsored by The Christian World Liberation Front on the University of California campus, June 22, 1971.
20. At a "Bible Rap" sponsored by the J.C. Light and Power House, Westwood Calif., June 16, 1971.
21. "The Fundamentalist-Modernist Controversy, 1918–1930," *op. cit.,* p. 272. *Cf.* Leon Festinger, Henry W. Riecken, Stanley Schacter, *When Prophecy Fails* (New York: Harper Torchbooks, 1964), "a social and psychological study of a modern group that predicted the destruction of the world."
22. Ernst Troeltsch, *The Social Teaching of the Christian Churches,* Vol. II, trans. by Olive Wyon (New York: Macmillan, 1931), p. 443.
23. *Religious Sects, op. cit.,* pp. 26–27.
24. Thomas F. O'Dea, *The Sociology of Religion* (Englewood Cliffs, N.J.: Prentice-Hall, Inc., 1966), p. 69. See also H. Richard Niebuhr, *The Social Sources of Denominationalism* (New York: Henry Holt & Company, 1929).
25. "Fundamentalism," *A Handbook of Christian Theology* (New York: Living Age Book, 1958), p. 142.
26. *Ibid.*
27. Jerald C. Brauer, *Protestantism in America* (Philadelphia: The Westminster Press, 1965), pp. 216–217.
28. "The Thrust of the Radical Right," *Sermons in American History, op. cit.,* p. 415.
29. Jerald C. Brauer, *op. cit.,* p. 282.
30. Elmer T. Clark, *The Small Sects in America* (Nashville: Abingdon Press, 1965), p. 26.
31. For the history and development of the "pretribulationary premillennialism" or "dispensationalism" of the fundamentalists, see Sandeen, *The Roots of Fundamentalism;* C. Norman Kraus, *Dispensationalism in America* (Richmond: John Knox Press, 1958); George Eldon Ladd, *The Blessed Hope* (Grand Rapids, Mich.: Eerdmans, 1956); Charles C. Ryrie, *Dispensationalism Today* (Chicago: Moody Press, 1965).
32. "America used the atomic bomb at Hiroshima as an instrument for freedom. It worked. For just the same reason America should now use the atomic power at the present moment, if necessary. If she does not, she is failing her stewardship before God" (*Author of Liberty* [1946] as quoted by Erling Jorstad, *The Politics of Doomsday, Fundamentalists of the Far Right* [Nashville: Abingdon Press, 1970], pp. 147–148).
33. *Ibid.,* p. 176.
34. *Ibid.*
35. *Ibid.*
36. Harold O. J. Brown, *The Protest of a Troubled Protestant* (New Rochelle, N.Y.: Arlington House, 1969), pp. 72–73; Richard V. Pierard, *The Unequal Yoke: Evangelical Christianity and Political Conservatism* (Philadelphia: J. B. Lippincott Company, 1970).
37. Quoted by L. Harold DeWolf, *op. cit.,* pp. 43–44.
38. Cited by Harold John Ockenga, "Resurgent Evangelical Leadership," *Christianity Today,* October 10, 1960; included in *A Christianity To-*

day Reader, edited by Frank E. Gaebelein (New York: Meredith Press, 1966), pp. 133–134.

39. *Ibid.*, p. 135.
40. *Ibid.*
41. *Ibid.*, p. 137.
42. *Ibid.*, pp. 138–139.
43. "Civil Rights and Christian Concern," May 8, 1964; *A Christianity Today Reader, op. cit.*, pp. 202–203.
44. *Ibid.*, p. 203.
45. See Lowell D. Streiker, *The Jesus Trip, Advent of the Jesus Freaks* (Nashville: Abingdon Press, 1971).
46. *20 Years Under God, op. cit.*, p. 11.

4

Fundamentalism and Middle America

To describe what Americans believe about God, about what is right and wrong, about what it means to be an American, is to describe Middle America. As Will Herberg maintains,[1] "The American Way of Life is a middle-class way, just as the American people in their entire outlook and feelings are a middle-class people." The notion of a "middle-class people" must strike some as an anomaly. For it may be asked whether the working classes of any nation may be described as "middle-class" in the same sense as either the "old middle classes"—farmers, craftsmen, artisans, small manufacturers, self-employed professional men, etc.—or the "new middle classes"—white collar office workers, managers, technicians, members of the mass media, public welfare, and service professions. Some authorities on class stratification have adopted the notion of a gradual *embourgeoisement* of Western industrial societies, the progressive adoption by the working class as a whole of middle-class standards and patterns of life. For example, T. B. Bottomore detects a "new social perspective" which regards labor union collectivism as a means, but no longer an end in itself. As the worker achieves the benefits of collective bargaining, his sense of solidarity with his class diminishes and he begins to withdraw into a private life characterized by "the individual worker's predominant concern with his family's standard of living, his own prospects of advancement, the education of his children and their opportunities to enter superior occupations." [2]

No nation has been more thoroughly *embourgeoised* than the United States. As Herberg has commented on his own brief summary of the values embodied in the American Way of Life: "It will not escape the reader that this account is essentially an idealized description of the middle-class ethos." [3] Americans possess a basic set of precepts about the nature of reality, the good life, and our national destiny, which stand alongside the creeds of the churches as a source of personal motivation and social norms. The overwhelmingly middle-class character of the churches came as something of a surprise to sociologists Rodney Stark and Charles Y. Glock. As a result of in-depth interviews with three thousand church members in Northern California, they discovered that "in contrast with the general public, church members are an extraordinarily affluent group; the poor are conspicuously absent from the church rolls. Even in the fundamentalist sects, traditionally thought to be the special havens of the poor, the majority of members are financially comfortable." Whether we use income or social and political attitudes as an index of *embourgeoisement,* we find conclusively that "church membership is predominantly a middle-class affair." [4]

But not only is church membership distinctively middle class, it is surprisingly fundamentalistic. The religious convictions of the majority of Americans are compatible to a remarkable degree to the cardinal doctrines of evangelical Protestantism. Also, at a time when the major mainline denominations are on the decline in terms of finances and social influence, conservative sects and denominations seem to be growing at a prodigious rate and clearly possess a vitality and self-confidence absent from American life in general and the American churches in particular.

SURVEYING THE FIELD

A prominent rabbi notes:

> Some are certain that religion in America is in eclipse, the hapless victim of an overwhelmingly secular environment. Others, defenders of the faith, sense the threat of such possibilities, rush out to survey the field, and, returning with a sigh of relief, manage to report that "99 per cent of you and your neighbors believe in God!" [5]

The present chapter is based on the findings of those who have rushed out to survey the field. Contrary to what the above-quoted critic suggests, the fact that "99 per cent of you and your neighbors believe in God" does not preclude the possibility that "religion in America is in eclipse." Before we decide what such statistical studies prove, we shall have to examine them. Polls, it should be remembered, represent what people *say* they believe and not necessarily what they "really" believe. Undoubtedly there is a tendency for people to respond to questions about their religious beliefs and observances according to what they feel they ought to respond or what they wish they could respond. But sincere or not, the fact that a respondent says, "I believe . . ." or "At least once a month I participate . . ." is highly significant. Of course, no poll is perfect. The way in which the questions are worded, the variety of alternatives available to the respondent, the circumstances under which the questions are asked, even the facial expression of the pollster, definitely influences the results. None of the polls upon which this chapter is based were crude in technique or totally insensitive to the ambiguities of the questions asked. Although better questions could be prepared, we are convinced that much can be learned from these questionnaire surveys.

In 1965 a Gallup poll was undertaken to "measure the religious beliefs and practices of American adults, and attitudes of members of the three main religious groups toward each other," and to determine what changes, if any, had occurred since a similar study made by Ben Gaffin and Associates in 1952. Sponsored by *The Catholic Digest,* the 1965 study was based on 2783 personal interviews conducted with a representative cross-section of U.S. adults 18 years of age and over. The entire study is included in the volume, *What Do We Believe? The Stance of Religion in America.*

The Glock-Stark survey was based on "an elaborate questionnaire study of church members in Northern California, and a national sample of adult Americans." The responses of 3,000 people who completed a detailed questionnaire for sociologists Charles Y. Glock and Rodney Stark in 1963 provide a valuable picture of the religious beliefs and practices of American church members. In 1964 many of the items from the Northern California survey were included in interviews conducted with a representative sample of the entire American adult population by National Opinion Research Center. Although there are some slight differences between the two studies, we have used the more elaborate Northern California church-member poll as the basis for the data presented in this chapter.[6]

Glock and Stark categorize the denominational identities of their respondents as Congregational, Methodist, Episcopal, Disciples of Christ, Presbyterian, American Baptist, American Lutheran, Missouri Lutheran, Southern Baptist, Sects, or Roman Catholic. The designation "Sects" includes the following groups: Assemblies of God, Church of Christ, Church of God, Foursquare Gospel, Free Methodist, Mennonite, Nazarene, Pentecostal, Salvation Army, Seventh-Day Adventist, Campbellite, Jehovah's Witnesses, Christian Missionary Alliance, Mission Covenant, and various small holiness bodies. Excluded are such "cults" as Christian Science, Unity, Theosophy, Spiritualism, and Divine Science; as well as Eastern Orthodoxy, the Church of the Latter-Day Saints (Mormons), and Asian religions. Our use of the term "sect" in the following pages conforms to Glock and Stark.

According to the 1965 Gallup survey of Americans eighteen years of age or older, there are 78.9 million Protestants, 29.8 Roman Catholics, 3.2 million Jews, a half million classified as "other," and 8.1 million with no religious preference. At the time of this poll, the American adult population stood at 120.5 million, and the total U.S. population at 194.6 million. Since 1965 our national population has grown by nearly nine million. In November 1971 a later Gallup poll estimated our voting age population (eighteen years of age and older) at 131 million.[7]

When we compare the 1965 Gallup figures with statistics gleaned from a similar poll conducted in 1952 by Ben Gaffin and Associates, we discover Catholic gains of 6 million, Protestant gains of nearly 8 million, slight decreases among Jews and those classified as "other," and an increase of 3 million in those declaring no religious preference.

According to the U.S. Bureau of Census figures, the 1952 adult population (eighteen years of age or older) was 107 million. Hence, the increase in the adult population between 1952 and 1965 was roughly 13 per cent. During the same period, the number of adult Americans indicating Protestant or Catholic religious preference grew by about 15 per cent (adult Protestants approximately 11 per cent; adult Catholics approximately 25 per cent). Thus the commonly held assumption that religion is not keeping pace with the growth of the population appears discredited. While it is true that over-all Protestant growth has fallen slightly behind the rate of adult population growth, Catholicism seems to have outgrown the adult population by a margin of two to one. The number and percentage of adults indicating a preference for Judaism has declined. At the same time, Americans indicating no religious preference increased at a rate three times as large as the growth of the adult population.

The distribution of Protestants within their various denominations and sects has shown definite patterns of change. The big gainers have been the Baptists with a growth of 5.6 million. Jehovah's Witnesses advanced from 200,000 to 500,000, and the Disciples of Christ from 200,000 to 400,000. During the same period, slight declines were posted by the Methodists, Lutherans, Presbyterians, Reformed, and Friends

(Quakers). It may be surmised that most of the Baptist increase belongs to the Southern Baptists.

AMERICA'S RELIGIOUS CONVICTIONS

What do Americans believe? First, they believe in God. Eighty-one per cent are "absolutely certain there is a God." An additional 12 per cent are "fairly sure." And only 2 per cent do not believe in God at all.

But what sort of God do Americans profess? A loving heavenly Father who looks after his children? Or some kind of impersonal, supernatural force such as destiny, progress, or Being-itself? According to the 1965 Gallup survey, 73 per cent think of God as "a loving Father who looks after us"; and only 19 per cent view him as "some kind of supernatural power."

The Glock-Stark survey of church members reveals that 71 per cent of the total Protestants affirm, "I know God really exists and I have no doubts about it." Another 17 per cent of the Protestants confess, "While I have doubts, I feel that I do believe in God." The Roman Catholic responses indicate that 81 per cent completely believe; while 13 per cent admit some doubts.

Placing the various religious groups in a continuum from least totally convinced to most convinced in the existence of God, we observe the following pattern:

I know God really exists
and I have no doubts about it

Jewish 39%
Congregational 41%
Methodist 60%
Episcopal 63%
American Lutheran 73%
Presbyterian 75%
Disciples of Christ 76%
American Baptist 78%
Missouri Lutheran 81%
Roman Catholic 81%

Sects 96%
Southern Baptist 99%

It is also significant that no religious group contains more than a slight number of atheists. The Congregationalists, one per cent of whom responded "I don't believe in God," lead all Christian groups. (The total for all Protestant groups was less than half of one per cent; and nil for Catholics. Yet atheism among Jews grew in the period between the two Gallup polls from one to 9 per cent.)

But not only are the vast majority of Americans theists; they are trinitarian theists at that. A full 83 per cent replied affirmatively to the question: "Do you believe in the Trinity—the Father, Son and Holy Ghost." Nearly all the Roman Catholics and Protestants polled by Gallup so affirmed (96 per cent and 86 per cent, respectively).

Second, Americans believe in Jesus. Only one per cent doubt that Jesus Christ ever actually lived. A striking 72 per cent (88 per cent of the Catholics and 73 per cent of the Protestants) believe that Jesus is God. Only 13 per cent claim that he is "just another religious leader like Mohammed or Buddha." Glock and Stark discovered that 69 per cent of the Protestant church members and 86 per cent of the Roman Catholics assert "Jesus is the Divine Son of God and I have no doubts about it." The pattern was as follows:

Jesus is the Divine Son of God
and I have no doubts about it

Congregational 40%
Methodist 54%
Episcopalian 59%
Presbyterian 72%
Disciples of Christ 74%
American Lutheran 74%
American Baptist 76%
Roman Catholic 86%
Missouri Lutheran 93%
Sects 97%
Southern Baptist 99%

Glock and Stark included three additional questions regarding christology: *Do you believe that Jesus was born of a virgin? Do you believe that Jesus walked on water? Do you believe Jesus will actually return to the earth some day?* A majority of the total Protestants (57 per cent) and most of the Roman Catholics (81 per cent) replied that the virgin birth of Jesus was "completely true." Half the Protestants and 71 per cent of the Catholics said that it was "completely true" that Jesus walked on water. Not quite half the respondents (44 per cent of the Protestants and 47 per cent of the Catholics) believe that Jesus will "definitely" return to earth. In addition, 10 per cent of the Protestants and Catholics believed that Christ's return was probable; 20 per cent of the Protestants and 16 per cent of the Catholics said that it is possible. Only one-tenth of the Protestants and one-eighth of the Catholics believe that Jesus will "definitely not" return. It would appear from these data that the vast majority of Americans do not reject the possibility that Jesus will actually return to earth in the future. The range of orthodoxy from group to group was as follows:

Jesus was born of a virgin
(Percentage who said "completely true")

Congregationalist 21%
Methodist 34%
Episcopalian 39%
Presbyterian 57%
Disciples of Christ 62%
American Lutheran 66%
American Baptist 69%
Roman Catholic 81%
Missouri Lutheran 92%
Sects 96%
Southern Baptist 99%

Jesus walked on water
(Percentage who said "completely true")

Congregational 19%
Methodist 26%

Episcopalian 30%
Presbyterian 51%
American Lutheran 58%
Disciples of Christ 62%
American Baptist 62%
Roman Catholic 71%
Missouri Lutheran 83%
Sects 94%
Southern Baptist 99%

Jesus will actually return to the earth some day
(Percentage who answered "definitely")

Congregationalist 13%
Methodist 21%
Episcopalian 24%
Disciples of Christ 36%
Presbyterian 43%
Roman Catholic 47%
American Lutheran 54%
American Baptist 57%
Missouri Lutheran 75%
Sects 89%
Southern Baptists 94%

We may conclude that *the convictions of most Americans regarding the existence of God and the person of Jesus Christ are quite compatible with the doctrines of fundamentalism,* i.e. There is a God; He watches over the lives of his children; He was present in the world in the person of Jesus of Nazareth; Jesus was born of a virgin, He is the divine Son of God, the worker of miracles. Fundamentalists are more certain than other Christians that Jesus will return to earth. But even though non-fundamentalists are not definitely convinced of the Second Coming, they allow for the possibility.

But what do Americans believe about the Bible? Do they consider it the divinely inspired Word of God or only a masterpiece of ancient literature written by a number of more or less fallible human beings over many generations. According to the 1965 Gallup poll, nearly four-fifths (79 per cent) classified the Bible as "the revealed word of God"; while only 13 per cent judged it to be "only a great piece of literature." More than half the Protestant and three-quarters of Catholic church members surveyed by Glock and Stark declared that "miracles actually happened just as the Bible says they did." The biblical miracles were doubted or rejected by only 17 per cent of the total Protestants and 9 per cent of the Catholics. With regard to the Bible, the majority of Americans hold convictions which are consonant with the basic doctrines of fundamentalism.

Moreover, three-quarters of all Americans answered in the affirmative when asked, "Do you think your soul will live on after death?" Only a tenth of those polled by Gallup and an even smaller percentage of those studied by Glock and Stark indicate that they doubt or reject the validity of life after death. But not only do Americans accept the concept of an afterlife; they believe in the eternal punishment of sinners and endless bliss of the righteous. Sixty-eight per cent of those polled by Gallup (including 71 per cent of the Protestant total and 80 per cent of the Catholics) answered *yes* to the question, "Do you think there is a Heaven, where people who have led good lives are eternally rewarded?" To the question, "Do you think there is a Hell, to which people who have led bad lives and die without being sorry are eternally damned?" more than half replied affirmatively (54 per cent of both the national total and the Protestant total; 70 per cent of the Roman Catholics).

Salvation—"Christianity's central concern and promise"—was a focal point of the Glock-Stark research. Explored by the two sociologists were beliefs and acts considered necessary requirements for salvation as well as improper beliefs and conducts which would be viewed as grounds for exclusion from salvation. Nearly two-thirds of the Protestants and more than half the Roman Catholics maintain that "belief in Jesus Christ as Saviour" is "absolutely necessary" for salvation (65 and 51 per cent respectively). Fifty-two per cent of the Protestants and 38 per cent of the Catholics claim that

members of these three groups believe that being Jewish could prevent salvation (53 per cent of Southern Baptists; 54 per cent of Missouri Lutherans; and 56 per cent of members of Sects). An even larger percentage felt that being a Hindu could prevent salvation (56 per cent of Missouri Lutherans; 59 per cent of Southern Baptists; and 68 per cent of the Sect members).

AMERICA'S RITUAL COMMITMENTS

When we turn from what Americans *believe* to the manner in which they *practice* their religion, we find that there exists a sizable gap between affirmations and actions. Seven out of every ten Americans interviewed told Gallup that they considered religion "very important" in their lives (74 per cent of the Protestants, 76 per cent of the Catholics). Yet only 38 per cent claimed that they attended church every week (33 per cent of the Protestants, 67 per cent of the Catholics). Almost as many never attend (a third of the Protestants, a seventh of the Catholics).

The Glock-Stark survey of church members confirms the Gallup figures for weekly attendance. According to their data, 36 per cent of the Protestants and 70 per cent of the Roman Catholics attend church every week. But among church members the percentage which "never" attends worship services drops to a scant one per cent for Protestants and 2 per cent for Catholics. When those who attend "nearly every week" are added to the "every week" worshippers, the results are arresting. Nearly two thirds of the total Protestants and eight-tenths of the Catholics attend worship services nearly every week or better. Add to these data, the number who attend at least once a month, and the total includes 84 per cent of the Protestants and 87 per cent of the Catholics. If Americans tell the truth about their attendance at religious services, they are assuredly the most faithful worshippers in the history of Christendom. It is clear from both surveys that among American adults in general (the Gallup Poll) and church members in particular (Glock-Stark), Americans who do not attend church regularly—once a month or more—constitute a minority! A breakdown of the figures by religious grouping duplicates the pattern seen above: Congregationalists are the least frequent in attendance (45 per cent attend nearly weekly or better; 78 per cent at least once a month); while the Sects, Southern Baptists, and the Missouri Lutherans can boast *weekly* percentages of 80, 59, and 43, respectively. More than 90 per cent of the members of these three groupings attend at least once a month.

Even if we accept the church attendance figures, there are reasons for suspecting that the piety of Americans is more ceremonial than personal. As we have seen, nearly 80 per cent of all Americans believe that the Bible is the revealed Word of God. Yet only 14 per cent read it "practically every day"; and 27 per cent admit they "never" or "practically never" read it. Similarly, although most Americans believe in life after death, few of them let their belief interfere with the quest for the "good life." Gallup asked, "Which do you think you should be most serious about—trying to live comfortably, or preparing for a life after death?" Forty-eight per cent of the total (46 per cent of the Catholics and 53 per cent of the Protestants) replied, "preparing for a life after death." One-quarter opted for living comfortably (21 per cent of the Catholics; 22 per cent of the Protestants). Thus, more than twice as many Americans believe that concern with an afterlife *should be* of paramount importance as those who believe that life in the present world should have precedence.

But, as is often the case in religious matters, there is a discrepancy between what *is* and what *should be*. Gallup asked the same sample, "Which do you think you yourself are most serious about—trying to live comfortably or preparing for a life after death?" The distribution of responses to this question virtually reverses the replies to the previous question. Nearly half admitted that they are more serious about trying to live comfortably (46 per cent of the total; 47 per cent of the Catholics and 42 per cent of the Protestants). Only one-fifth claimed that preparing for an afterlife was of greater importance (13 per cent of the Catholics; 24 per cent of the Protestants).

Selecting regular attendance at worship services and grace before meals as ritual acts which would be encouraged by all Christian groups, Glock and Stark constructed a "ritual index" to measure commitment. They discovered:

> In a sample of persons, *all* of whom were formal members of specific congregations and parishes, the Christian churches generally fail to meet the standard of universal ritual commitment; *indeed the majority of Protestants and Catholics fail to fulfill even these minimal standards of ritual commitment.*[8]

Glock and Stark ranked their respondents "low," "medium," or "high." A person was classified as "high" if he or she *both* attended church every, or nearly every, week *and* said grace at least once a week. A person who performed either of these obligations during the specified period was ranked "medium." The remainder were classified "low." While only 44 per cent of the Protestants and 46 per cent of the Catholics placed high on the index, it is significant that five Protestant groups did: Sects with 87 per cent, Southern Baptists with 68 per cent, American Baptists with 57 per cent, Missouri Lutherans with 53 per cent, and American Lutherans with 51 per cent. The percentages for the other Protestant groups were as follows: Disciples of Christ, 40; Presbyterian, 39; Methodist, 32; Episcopalian, 30; and Congregational, 22.

THE THREE CAMPS: LIBERALS, MODERATES, CONSERVATIVES

When we examine the *total* responses (i.e., total Americans, total Protestants, total church members), we are impressed by the extremely conservative character of American religion. After all, 93 per cent of the total adult population are absolutely or fairly sure of the existence of God; 83 per cent accept the Trinity; 72 per cent say that Jesus was God; 79 per cent regard the Bible as the revealed Word of God, and so forth. But, as we have seen, when the figures are broken down according to the various denominational or sectarian groups, we discover that there are great differences on nearly every issue. (This is not to deny that there is often extreme difference of opinion within certain groups, e.g. the Methodists.) In general, the American religious groups listed by Glock and Stark can readily be separated into three attitudinal camps: *a*) liberals (Congregationalists, Methodists, and Episcopalians); *b*) moderates (Disciples, Presbyterians, American Lutherans, and American Baptists); and *c*) conservatives (Missouri Lutherans, Southern Baptists, Sectaries, and Roman Catholics).

If we remove the Catholics from the picture so that we may concentrate our attention upon American Protestantism, we find that the distribution of adult Americans according to out tentative groupings is as follows: liberals—22 million; moderates—28 million; and conservatives—23 million. These figures are based on the several sources. We have compared U.S. Census statistics with the various surveys mentioned above as well as with the membership records of the various denominations and sects.

Much the same picture of division of American Protestants into conservative, moderate, and liberal groups emerges from a 1957 poll of American ministers conducted by the Opinion Research Corporation for *Christianity Today*.[9] Each minister was asked: "Just how would you generally classify your theological position—fundamentalist, conservative, neo-orthodox, liberal, or some other category?" The breakdown of responses:

Theological Position of American Ministers

Conservative 39%
Fundamentalist 35%
Liberal 14%
Neo-orthodox 12%

The fact that 41 per cent of the self-professed "conservative" clergymen indicated that it was not essential to preach and teach "the Bible as having been verbally inspired by God in original writings" suggests a definite gap between them and the fundamentalists, on the one hand, and the liberals and neo-orthodox, on the other. (Only 25 per cent of the neo-orthodox and 23 per cent of the liberal respondents considered it essential to preach and teach this doctrine.) Finally, we would add that it is not unlikely that the ministers of the group which we designate "moderate" (Disciples, Presbyterians, American Lutherans, and American Baptists) would consider themselves "conservative,"—indeed it is likely that the adult membership of the same denominations would also declare themselves "conservative" if they were given only the four options of the *Christianity Today* poll.

Allowing for the imprecision of our designations, what generalizations can be made about the three groups?

Liberal Protestantism

The liberal Protestant rates low in orthodox belief. Compared to the total Protestants, 71 per cent of whom have no doubts of the existence of God, only 41 per cent of Congregational church members, 60 per cent of Methodists, and 63 per cent of Episcopalians claim such complete confidence. (Unless otherwise noted all percentages are based on the Glock-Stark church-member sample. Where three figures appear in parentheses in the following discussion, the first refers to the percentage of Congregational church members, the second to Methodist church members, and the third to Episcopalian church members.) Although 69 per cent of all church members believe in the divinity of Jesus, only about half of the liberals do (40, 54, 59). Similarly few liberals (13, 21, 24) believe that Jesus will definitely return to earth or that the devil exists (6, 13, 17). Two-thirds of the general Protestant total thinks that belief in Jesus as savior is necessary for salvation; but only a minority of the liberals concur (38, 45, 47). Rated on an orthodoxy index based on beliefs in life after death, the virgin birth of Jesus, whether or not Jesus walked on water, and original sin, one-third of the total Protestants were scored high by Glock and Stark; but few of the liberals were (4, 10, 14). Conversely, while only 18 per cent of all Protestants were scored low, nearly half the Congregational church members, 30 per cent of the Methodists, and 24 per cent of the Episcopalians did not believe even one of the four doctrines mentioned.

Although they rate low in orthodoxy, the liberals placed much greater emphasis on the importance of man's relationships with his fellows than did most moderate and conservative groups. As Glock and Stark comment, "There is a slight tendency for Protestants to be either orthodox and nonethical, or ethical and unorthodox" in their over-all religious orientations.[10] When asked how sure they are that they have found "the answers to the meaning and purpose of life," 56 per cent of the Protestants were quite certain that they had either grown up knowing these things or had definitely found the answers at a later time. Fewer than half the liberals expressed such certainty (39, 42, 45).

We have noted the high attendance figures boasted by all American churches (63 per cent of the Protestant church members attend services "nearly weekly or better"). But liberals lag in this respect as well (45, 51, 56). We have seen that most Christian groups are rated less than high on Glock and Stark's ritual commitment index (church members who *both* attend church nearly weekly or better and who say grace at least once a week were classified as high). Liberal percentages of those rated high (22, 32, 30) were much lower than even the mediocre total Protestant result (44 per cent classified as high). Liberals read the Bible less often than other Protestants (46 per cent of the total Protestants read the Bible frequently, but fewer than a third—20, 29, and 30 per cent—of the liberals do).

Liberals are less likely to believe in the efficacy of prayer, less likely to have ever experienced the presence of God, a sense of salvation through Christ, or a sense of having been punished by God than are other Christians. In fact, nearly one-quarter of them (28, 18, 20) have had neither salvation experiences nor experiences of the presence of God during their entire adult lives. Although a third of the total Protestant church members feel that they have had experiences of temptation, most of the liberal have not (11, 16, 24).

Two separate indices suggest that the liberal level of religious knowledge is exceedingly low. A Glock-Stark scale of religious knowledge based on the respondent's ability to recognize quotations from the Bible and to select the names of Old Testament prophets rates as high only 27 per cent of the over-all Protestant total. But liberal scores were even worse (17, 16, 17). A Gallup survey conducted in 1954 found that only 36 per cent of the Protestants knew who preached the Sermon on the Mount; 32 per cent could name the founder of one religion other than Christianity; only 21 per cent could name two major Old Testament prophets; 22 per cent knew the author of the most books in the New Testament; and 35 per cent were aware of the country that ruled Jerusalem during the time of Jesus.[11] Although the Gallup data are not divided into denominational groups, we can expect that the liberal Protestants would possess even less religious knowledge than the general Protestant population.

One area in which the Congregationalists, Methodists, and Episcopalians cannot be considered "liberal" is in the financial support of their churches. When the various Christian groups are ranked according to percentage of members with annual incomes of $10,000 or more, the order is:

Members with Incomes of $10,000 or More

Congregational 64%
Methodist 52%
Presbyterian 48%
Episcopalian 47%
Disciples of Christ 46%
American Lutheran 44%
Missouri Lutheran 41%

American Baptist 39%
Roman Catholic 34%
Southern Baptist 26%
Sects 22%

But when we rank the same groups according to the percentage which contributes at least $7.50 a week to their church, it turns out that there is no relationship between affluence and church giving:

Percentage of members who contribute at least $7.50 a week

Southern Baptist 59%
Sects 56%
American Baptist 39%
Disciples of Christ 38%
Missouri Lutheran 26%
American Lutheran 24%
Presbyterian 20%
Episcopalian 18%
Methodist 18%
Congregational 15%
Roman Catholic 6%

Thus, it turns out that the two groups with the fewest affluent members (Sects and Southern Baptist) contribute the most heavily, while the four Protestant denominations with the largest percentage of affluent members (Congregational, Methodist, Presbyterian, and Episcopalian) are the most niggardly.

The membership of liberal churches constitute "religious audiences" rather than primary groups which provide a focus for their members' day-by-day activities. Glock and Stark asked church members, "Of five best friends, how many belong to your congregation?" More than a quarter (29 per cent) of all Protestants reported that three to five of their closest friends were members of their congregations. The liberals lagged behind (18, 24, 20). In fact, half of the Congregationalists reported that none of their closest friends belonged to their local churches. (Percentages of Methodists and Episcopalians who replied "none" were 43 and 39, respectively; among the total Protestants, 36). The liberal church members do appear to be vigorous "joiners." Nine-tenths of the Congregationalists and Methodists belong to at least one voluntary organization (fraternal groups, service clubs, political groups, farm organizations, etc.). Congregationalists are more than three times as likely to belong to four or more voluntary organizations as either Southern Baptists or sect members. But conversely, conservative Christians are more likely to restrict their activities to their local congregations. Liberal Christians have a much greater number of social involvements, and perhaps as a result are more likely to regard the activities of their local congregations as of secondary importance. In sum, liberal church members provide the warm bodies and cash support needed by all social and political causes. But their dedication to institutional religion is of such little importance to them; their orthodoxy and ritual commitments rank so low; the percentage of their incomes devoted to their churches is so small; their religious knowledge is so scanty—that they cannot be counted upon either to maintain the requisite personal and corporate expressions of traditional religion in America (e.g. personal piety, local congregations, denominational programs) or to exert a distinctively Christian influence upon American society in general.

Moderate Protestantism

The position of the moderates has already been examined, for they are the average Protestants reported on earlier. In most particulars, the members of the Disciples of Christ (the Christian Church), Presbyterians, American Lutherans (the American Lutheran Church and the Lutheran Church in America), and American Baptists (non-Southern Baptists) stand within a few percentage points of the statistics for total Protestants. For example, 26 per cent of the total Protestants report annual incomes of $6,000 or less; the percentages for the four moderate groups were as follows: Disciples, 24;

Presbyterians, 23; American Lutherans, 28; and American Baptists, 26.

If we could break down our data into the various denominations which are included in the designations Presbyterian and American Baptist such as the United Presbyterian Church in the U.S.A., Presbyterian Church in the United States (the so-called "Southern Presbyterians"), the American Baptist Convention, Negro Baptists, the Conservative Baptist Association of America, etc., we would definitely discover liberal-conservative polarities within each group. But then again, we could divide even the most liberal or conservative denominations into several ideological camps.

Conservative Protestantism

Conservative Protestant church members "know God really exists and . . . have no doubts about it." So declare 81 per cent of the Missouri Lutherans, 99 per cent of the Southern Baptists, and 96 per cent of the sect members. (Where three figures appear in parentheses in the following discussion, the first refers to the percentage of Missouri Lutherans, the second to Southern Baptists, and the third to sect members.) They are even more convinced that Jesus is God (93, 99, 97). They believe that Jesus will actually return to earth (75, 94, 89), and that the devil really exists (77, 92, 90). They are positive that acceptance of Jesus as savior is essential for redemption (97, 97, 96); are fairly certain that being ignorant of Jesus will definitely or possibly prevent salvation (64, 80, 78 as compared with 39 per cent of the total Protestants). A majority of conservative Christians assert that being Jewish is an obstacle to salvation (54, 53, 56)—a percentage which is more than twice the figure for Protestants in general (25 per cent).

The conservative Protestants outscored the general Protestant population on the Glock-Stark orthodoxy index. A third of the total Protestants were rated high as compared to two-thirds or more of the conservatives (66, 88, 86). While 18 per cent of the total Protestants were scored low, virtually none of the conservatives were (1, 0, 1). Conservative Protestants have a tendency to consider their relationship with God more important than their relationships with their fellow men. They are quite convinced that they have "found the answers to the meaning and purpose of life." Most of them either "grew up knowing these things" (43, 44, 49) or are now "quite certain, although at one time I was pretty uncertain" (27, 46, 36). It is perhaps surprising that the sect members and the Southern Baptists, groups which stress the need for personal crisis conversion and believer's baptism, include such large percentages of members who have never doubted the truth of their faith. It would appear that among conservative Protestants only the Southern Baptists contain more converts than members who have grown up in the faith (46 and 44 per cent, respectively).

On matters of faith, the three conservative Protestant groups (Missouri Lutherans, Southern Baptists, and Sects) are virtually indistinguishable. Further, there is a definite gap between them and the moderate camp. Although the percentage of Missouri Lutherans scored high by Glock and Stark on their orthodoxy index was only 66 per cent compared to 88 and 86 per cent of the Southern Baptists and sect members, no moderate group came within 23 per cent (43 per cent of the American Lutherans and American Baptists were ranked high). And only one per cent of Missouri Lutherans were ranked low in orthodoxy as compared with 12 to 16 per cent of the moderates (Disciples, 16 per cent; Presbyterians, 16; American Lutherans, 13; American Baptists, 12).

But on matters of religious observance, experience, and knowledge, the highly orthodox Missouri Lutherans often fell behind the "moderate" American Baptists. The American Baptists have a higher percentage of regular Bible readers—54 per cent as compared to 46 per cent of the Missouri Lutherans; slightly exceed the Missouri Lutherans in percentage of members who have experienced the presence of God (50 and 49 per cent, respectively), and salvation in

Christ (56 and 52 per cent). Both the American Baptists and the Disciples of Christ outscored the Missouri Lutherans by a considerable extent on the Glock-Stark religious knowledge index (40 per cent of the Disciples and 30 per cent of the American Baptists were scored high, but only 23 per cent of the Missouri Lutherans). In addition, both Disciples and American Baptists had greater percentages of their members with three to five of their closest friends drawn from their own congregations (42 per cent of the Disciples, 40 per cent of the American Lutherans, 25 per cent of the Missouri Lutherans); and fewer members with no close friends in their own congregations (Disciples, 36 per cent; American Baptists, 31; Missouri Lutherans, 40).

We should remember not only that the Missouri Lutherans have a different national, historical, theological, and liturgical ancestry from the Southern Baptist and the Sects, but they include in their ranks a much higher percentage of members with annual incomes of $10,000 or more than do the other conservative groups. Conversely, the percentage of sect members with annual incomes of $6,000 or less is nearly twice the percentage for Missouri Lutherans.[12]

If we compare all three of the conservative groups with the averages for all Protestants, however, we find that the conservatives attend church with greater regularity (63 per cent of the total Protestants attend nearly weekly or better; the conservative percentages are 73, 84, and 93); rank higher in ritual commitment (44 per cent of the total Protestants were scored high; the conservatives: 53, 68, 87); and include as many or more regular Bible readers (46 per cent of the total Protestants; 46 per cent of Missouri Lutherans; 86 per cent of the Southern Baptists; and 89 per cent of the sect members). Their belief in prayer and regularity of prayer earned them higher scores (63, 85, 83) on the Glock-Stark devotionalism index than the general Protestant score (53). They outranked the total Protestants in religious experience as well. More of the conservatives have experienced the presence of God, have undergone salvation experiences, have felt that God was at some time in their lives punishing them for previous sins or that the devil was tempting them. Virtually no conservatives were ranked low on the Glock-Stark religious experience index (3, 0, 0); while 14 per cent of the total Protestants were. The vast majority were ranked high on the same index (76, 97, 94), as compared to 58 per cent of the total Protestants.

With the exception of the Missouri Lutherans, the conservatives appear twice as knowledgeable in religious matters as the Protestant average. More than half of the Southern Baptists and sect members (51 and 69 per cent) were ranked high on the religious knowledge index, but only 27 per cent of the Protestant total. Very large percentages of both Southern Baptists and sect members reported that three to five of their closest friends were members of their churches (49 per cent of the Southern Baptists, 67 per cent of the sect members); and very few said that none of their close friends belonged to their congregations (23 and 9 per cent). Glock and Stark found that they were more likely to be involved in religious than secular organizations. More than 40 per cent of the Southern Baptist and sect members reported that 60 per cent or more of the organizations to which they belonged were religious. This degree of involvement in mostly religious organizations is more than double the over-all Protestant average of 19 per cent. In fact, large numbers of conservatives (17 per cent of the Missouri Lutherans, 16 per cent of the Southern Baptists, and 22 per cent of the sect members) limit their participation solely to church organizations. In many respects, conservative churches are primary groups characterized by "face-to-face association, intimacy, . . . small numbers of persons involved, and relative permanence." [13] It is in such groups that the individual forms his basic convictions about his world and himself. It is the decline of such groups in numbers and importance which has produced the loneliness, alienation, and boredom of modern urban life.

THE GROWTH OF FUNDAMENTALISM

According to all indications, conservative-fundamentalist denominations and sects are growing at a rate which exceeds the expansion of the mainline denominations or the rise of the general population. Between 1952 and 1965 the number of adults who claimed that they belonged to or preferred the Baptists increased by almost a third from 18 million to 23.6 million; [14] those who said they belonged to or preferred the Assemblies of God grew fivefold from two hundred thousand to one million; the Churches of God in Christ doubled from four hundred thousand to eight hundred thousand; the Church of the Nazarene showed a two-thirds increase from three hundred thousand to one-half million: Pentecostal Assemblies won two hundred thousand additional adherents, an increase of one-third. The combined growth of these five groups (7.2 million) nearly equals the total Protestant increase during the same years (7.8 million). From 1952 to 1965 the U.S. population grew by about 23 per cent. During the same period the number of adults indicating affiliation with or preference for the Methodists, Lutherans, Presbyterians, Reformed, and Friends declined. The number of Episcopalians increased slightly—by less than one per cent.[15]

As Albert Rasmussen commented over a decade ago,

> The really big upsurge in religious life in America is not to be found in the old-line and more staid denominations. . . . The majority in this upsurge are Biblical literalists. They make little or no attempt to relate their faith to modern culture. They represent a highly individualistic and moralistic view with little concern for the social, political and community processes.[16]

William G. McLoughlin estimates that the sixty "fringe-sect" groups in the United States—including pentecostal, holiness, and millenarian groups—have "increased their membership by 500 to 700 per cent over the past twenty years, while the traditional Protestant denominations and the Roman Catholic [Church] have increased by only 75 to 90 per cent, barely keeping up with the growth in population."[17] During the past years while denominational and interchurch programs have been collapsing for lack of interest or financial support; while theological seminary enrollments have been dropping; while the circulation of major Protestant periodicals has been plummeting; while laymen have remained unmoved by either social activism or ecumenism; while new religious books have been about as salable as week-old fish—the fundamentalists have been prospering. The circulation of devotional magazines has soared; several publishers including venerable J. B. Lippincott Company have been putting their eggs in the evangelical basket and have flourished thereby; firms which publish exclusively for fundamentalists have been hard-pressed to keep up with the demand for the writings of such conservative stalwarts as Keith Miller and Pat Boone; a revival of "old-fashioned" fundamentalism—the Jesus Freaks, street Christians, or Jesus People—is currently under way among the youth of California and shows every sign of spreading across the country; Billy Graham, who—with the death of Reinhold Niebuhr—has become the last big name in American religion, is consistently ranked among the three most admired Americans in national polls; fundamentalists have started a university (Oral Roberts), taken over a bankrupt liberal arts school (Mackinac College), and have assumed control of millions of dollars of real estate in the Cape Kennedy area which will soon be transformed into a college, conference center, and amusement park by the followers of Christian anti-Communist Carl McIntire.[18]

What accounts for this prodigious growth? What are the sources of this resurgence of fundamentalism? First, it has been suggested that fundamentalism provides comfort, support, and identity for adults in a mobile, rapidly changing, morally uncertain and bewildering culture. Fundamentalism is particularly attractive to urban newcomers. Rasmussen observes: "Displaced from the soil into an urban context, becoming dominated by vast organizations, feeling no sense of control over their own destiny, not fully sharing in the middle-class hope of upper mobility, uprooted people find a sense of belongingness and a new elite of the saved in which they can enroll themselves." [19] But the newly arrived immigrants from the soil to the city are not the only segment of our population attracted by the appeal of fundamentalism. There are others from all social classes who seek the simple answers of an idealized past as antidote to the emptiness, loneliness, confusion, and uncertainty of modern existence. For what is more emotionally exciting, personally involving, and deeply satisfying than the "old-time religion"? Where else can the urban newcomer and the disillusioned suburbanite find inner motivation to meet the demands of conventional middle-class morality in a rapidly changing world? "It would seem," states Rasmussen, "that old-line Protestant groups have been lined up so strongly with the standard-maintaining function rather than the forgiving and grace-giving function that they have cut themselves off from dealing with people who have suffered any of the disorganizations that are so numerous amidst the cross tensions of the city." [20] The mainline churches stand for property ownership and prestige. Their handsome church structures celebrate the achievements of their members. But millions of Americans own little or nothing. These Americans turn to their churches not to commemorate their accomplishments but to assuage their fears. They look to their churches for unchanging realities to cling to as protection against forces which the individual can neither fathom nor control. The suburban Christian worships on Sunday, locks his sanctuary, and returns a week later to make sure that the surrounding neighborhood has not damaged his property. But fundamentalism is not enmeshed by the churches' "edifice complex." There are many cavernous fundamentalist churches, some with thousands of members; but there exist far more small undistinguished structures as well as the thousands of storefronts, schools, and private homes in which the faithful congregate. Perhaps such portable religion is better suited to a mobile population than the enormous, costly, fixed, pseudo-cathedrals of the established denominations.

The manner in which the mainline churches have exercised their *priestly* function, their support of a *status quo* which discriminates against the poor and the uneducated, is often adduced as a ground for fundamentalist success among the dispossessed. But the way in which the established churches have assumed their *prophetic* role has more decisively contributed to the apparent reinvigoration of conservative forces. Put bluntly, the social involvement of the mainline churches has proved a disaster. Those who turn to their church for solace and inspiration have been estranged by local, denominational, and interchurch programs which they found at best confusing and at worst repulsive.

In the words of a fireman whose son died in Viet Nam:

> You know what gripes me more than anything else? It's the clergy, the priests and ministers, who get sucked into this radical business. Ever since I was a kid the church was quiet on all these things; they never shouted at you about how bad the country is, and we're murdering millions of the colored and we're murdering in Asia. All of a sudden they switch their line on us. I grew up hearing on Sunday this was a great country; now I get a sermon that makes me think I'm living in one of the worst countries in the world. Now, what the hell is a guy supposed to make of all this? I ask you? What do some of those priests and their minister friends think we are, light switches, that you can turn on and off, just because they decide to? [21]

And another hardworking "Middle American" complains about his minister:

> To hear him talk on Sunday, you'd think we were on the verge of ruin, America, unless we solve every problem we have and especially the race problem. He's got the Negro people on his brain, our minister. He must dream about them every night. He says we're to blame, the white people, for all that's happened. I went up once after the sermon and asked him what I've done that's to blame. He said he didn't mean any one per-

son, just the whole white world. I didn't know how I could answer him. I said I'd never wanted to hurt a Negro, all I wanted was for them to leave me alone and I'd leave them alone. But that got him going again, and I pretended that I had to leave, because we had to be somewhere. On the way home I told Doris I'm ready to start shopping for a new church.[22]

Those who passionately support the various national and international policies promoted by the Church have found that there are more direct paths to the attainment of their goals. Once the activist has been energized by his religious community, he tends to find totally secular ways to express his concerns. The draining of activist money, time, and imagination away from the local, national, and international programs of the churches has done much to create the impression of a rightward drift of institutional American Christianity. In many areas, *e.g.* publishing, the conservative is taking over by default.[23]

The American fetish for education and the manner in which our children are educated may also account for the acceptability of fundamentalism. Our system of public education encourages conformity, social adjustment, self-control, and the faultless reproduction of "correct" answers. There is little room for imagination, personal insight, integration of diverse data, independent judgment, or the recognition of the essential ambiguity of the world.[24] As a nation we are fond of simple solutions and unequivocal answers. In the moral sphere we expect absolutes "sharply etched in black and white." We regard the universe as divided into forces of good and forces of evil just like a television Western. We are prone to forget too easily that "even a saint falls short of the Godhead, and even Satan, though fallen, is a fallen angel." [25] The high regard which Americans hold for education, and their inability to appreciate the ambiguities of existence enhance the appeal of religious fundamentalism. For fundamentalism offers objective answers (the Bible), simple answers (the world is divided into the saved and the unsaved), and easy answers (there is little that any fundamentalist sect considers essential which cannot be learned in a single day). And the acceptance of the fundamentalist answers confers what Americans most want from education: certainty, direction for life, and prestige. America's legendary anti-intellectualism is not so much disdain for education as impatience with the snail's-pace gradualism of the deliberative process. The fundamentalist promise of objective knowledge, certainty, and a direct remedy for complex personal and social problems is hard to resist.

But probably the greatest single reason for the growth of fundamentalism is the persistent decline in the habitual optimism of the American people.[26] According to the fundamentalist, everything is exactly as it should be. The disintegration of society, the public loss of confidence, the constant threats of war and natural calamity, the breakdown of traditional moral standards, the increase of violence, the apparent insurmountability of the problems which face the human race as a whole and every individual in particular—all that is as it should be. For Jesus is coming soon! We may accuse the fundamentalists of irresponsibility, of passively allowing evil to have its way. But at the same time we will have to admit that a sense of futility and despair has often overtaken us as we have earnestly sought the amelioration of present conditions. Where are the public men we admired? Dead by the hand of assassins, destroyed by their own failings, or proved villains by subsequent events. What difference has all our marching, chanting, organizing, and praying made?

As a general rule, *fundamentalism flourishes not when things are bad* (*e.g.* during the First and Second World Wars or the Depression), *but when it appears that they could get appreciably worse*. Catastrophe breeds courage, but the constant threat of catastrophe brings despair. When a society rejects the way things have been done in the past, but cannot find acceptable directions for the future, fundamentalism exerts its greatest appeal. Clearly, we are living in such a time. For the revolution of rising expectations which followed the Second World War, and the inability of our society to meet those expectations has produced a sense of personal powerlessness and frustration in the great majority of our citizens. Old assumptions have been discredited; new options appear unworkable. Only faith in the God of our fathers can save us now.

Finally, a principal reason for the current upswing of fundamentalism is the natural affinity between fundamentalist doctrine and the religious convictions of Americans in general. This should be compared with the conclusion reached a generation ago by W. W. Sweet that Protestants who belong to no church "are, as a whole, conservative, have more sympathy for fundamentalism than modernism, and are not slow to express their disapproval of what they call 'newfangled ideas.' "[27]

The following table compares the responses of the total adult population with those who identified their religious preference as "Other and None" (i.e., other than Protestant, Catholic, or Jew) in the Gallup Poll.

	Total	*Other and None*
Absolutely certain there is a God	81%	45%
Fairly certain there is a God	12%	20%
Active member of church or religious group	73%	5%
Never attend church	32%	81%
Attend once a month or more	58%	17%
Believe in the Trinity	83%	41%
Believe that Jesus was God	72%	33%
Believe that Bible is revealed Word of God	79%	41%
Never read Bible	16%	38%

Do not pray	8%	37%
Believe in life after death	75%	37%
Do not believe in life after death	10%	42%
Believe in heaven	68%	26%
Believe in hell	54%	20%
Received Sunday School training as a child	69%	66%
Received no religious training as a child	9%	21%
Would want child of mine to receive Sunday School training	71%	54%
Would want child of mine to receive no religious training	2%	13%

It is significant that although eight out of ten of the "Other and None" do not attend church, two-thirds are fairly or absolutely sure that God exists, two-fifths believe in the Trinity and the divine inspiration of the Scriptures, and one-third in the deity of Jesus. Two-thirds attended Sunday school as children, and a majority want their children to receive similar training. According to the same poll, adults in the "Other and None" category have an extremely high regard for local clergymen (89 per cent rated local clergyman "very outstanding"; only 65 per cent of the total adults agreed).

We would conclude from these data that unchurched Americans are not predisposed toward fundamentalism on the basis of their religious convictions. But this is not to deny that the tensions of the times and the widespread feeling of despair may propel the unchurched in the direction of fundamentalist groups whose doctrines have been previously validated by a broad consensus regarding what Americans believe. Fundamentalism seems a natural direction for the unchurched because it is in harmony with what most Americans affirm.

A breakdown of the "Other and None" statistics reveals

that two-thirds are men; half are between the ages of 25 and 44; four-fifths are white; three-quarters have more than a grade-school education; more than half are manual workers or unemployed; nearly half belong to the middle income bracket, 39 per cent are lower income, only 14 per cent are upper income. With the exception of the large percentage of men, the "unchurched" are remarkably like the population as a whole in all the above respects. In addition, the percentages of the "Other and None" living in large cities, small cities, and rural areas, respectively; and the percentages living in each of the various regions of the country are almost identical to the distribution of the general adult population. Other than the preponderance of men and the relative "heterodoxy" of their beliefs, the "unchurched" are typical Americans.

IS THERE A FUNDAMENTALIST BOOM?

Whether the growth of the conservative churches is more apparent than real is a serious question. For much of the evidence of this growth adduced above consists of "soft" indicators. All that they really demonstrate is that some people (journalists, publishers, churchmen, magazine subscribers, etc.) are acting or reacting as if there were a fundamentalist boom. A short time ago several soft indicators suggested, on the one hand, that God was dead, and, on the other, that the Roman Catholic Church was undergoing substantial reform as the result of the Second Vatican Council. Neither contention was empirically verified (or falsified). There is scant evidence of decline of belief in God among Americans in general. The fact that half the adult Catholics in America say they never heard of Vatican II casts some doubt upon the pervasiveness of the spirit of reformation. We are not attempting, however, to prove or disprove either hypothesis, but only to point out the danger of acting as if an unsubstantiated hypothesis were true. Whether or not so-called modern man has lost faith in God; whether or not the spirit of *aggorniomento* was inaugurated by Vatican II, the fact that these beliefs have been advocated, disputed, and debated has made a difference. Likewise, whether or not fundamentalism is on the rise, many influential people are already reacting as if it were, and their reactions can be expected to make a difference.

What are the facts of the matter? Membership figures reported annually to the National Council of Churches support the contention that conservative churches are growing faster than moderate and liberal bodies. But such figures are notoriously unreliable. Local congregations add members to their rolls without a careful examination of qualifications, but remove them only upon the gravest provocation. Hence, church rolls contain the names of the deceased and people who have been institutionalized or long since moved away, as well as of individuals who have joined other congregations. Since it is easier to add than to subtract members, last year's errors are added to this year's denomination-wide census. In this connection, Glock and Stark feel that "the conservative churches may have been celebrating a paper empire, . . . while they thought they were doing better than other denominations they may actually have been doing worse." [28]

The truth of the matter seems to be that fundamentalist churches are *gaining* and *losing* members at a faster rate than moderate and liberal denominations. The conservative churches have been singularly successful in winning the unchurched from among the lower socioeconomic strata. But as the members advance in income and social status, they tend to transfer their membership to moderate or liberal churches which, in turn, funnel their upwardly mobile members into political and social causes unrelated to church involvement.

Approximately half of the total membership of the U.S. House of Representatives and Senate as well as nearly half of the state governors are members of one of three Protestant denominations: Methodist, Episcopalian, and Presbyterian.

Yet these same groups comprise less than a quarter of the voting age population. The percentage of legislative seats and governorships held by members of these three denominations is exactly twice the percentage of Americans who belong to them. On the other hand, Baptists, who make up nearly one-fifth of the total U.S. population, hold only 12 per cent of the Senate seats, 10 per cent of the House seats, and 12 per cent of the governorships. Eastern Orthodoxy, Lutheranism, fundamentalist sects, and the unchurched are with little or no representation. As Edwin Gaustad states, ". . . the 36 per cent of America's [religiously] unaffiliated may argue that it is the most under-represented minority in the country."[29]

According to the 1965 Gallup poll, 80 per cent of all adult Americans have never changed religious affiliations. Most Americans have always been members of the religious groups to which they presently belong. Of the 20 per cent who reported that they had changed denominations, half did so because of marriage or because they moved to an area in which the church of their denomination was less conveniently located than the congregation of the denomination which they decided to join. Only one-fifth of the "switchers" changed church affiliation due to religious convictions.

Church Members Who Have Never Changed Religious Affiliation

Jewish 95%
Roman Catholic 91%
Baptist 85%
Methodist 80%
Lutheran 75%
Congregational 71%
Other Protestant denominations 68%
Presbyterian 66%
Episcopal 59%

It is apparent that the "liberal" Congregationalists and Episcopalians, as well as the "moderate" Presbyterians, win more converts than the "moderate-conservative" Baptists, despite the fact that the evangelistically inclined Southern Baptists comprise nearly half of the Baptists in America.

The Glock-Stark church member survey produced a slightly different picture. We should remember that Gallup interviewed a random sample representing the *entire adult* population. Eighty per cent of this general sample maintain that they have never changed their religious affiliation. But when *Protestant church members* are isolated, we discover that nearly half (46 per cent) say they have previously been members of a denomination other than the one to which they presently belong. Accordingly, the net percentage gain or loss in membership for each of the various Protestant denominations was as follows:

Net Gain or Loss in Membership

Congregational +2%
Methodist −17%
Episcopalian +40%
Disciples of Christ −32%
Presbyterian +22%
American Lutheran −5%
American Baptist −8%
Missouri Lutheran −5%
Southern Baptist −34%
Sects −9%

Thus, while Glock and Stark found that Protestants are much more likely to change denominations than the Gallup data might lead us to believe, the data of both surveys indicate that it is not the conservatives but the Episcopalians, Presbyterians, and Congregationalists who are gaining members. Indeed, it would appear that members are trickling at a slow but steady rate out of the Sects and the Missouri Lutherans (both "conservative"), the American Baptists and the American Lutherans (both "moderate"); and that they are leaving the conservative Southern Baptists as well as the moderate Disciples of Christ and the liberal Methodists at an alarming rate. According to Glock and Stark, liberals and moderates exchange members at roughly equivalent rates, while losing very few members to the conservatives. But the conservatives lose a considerable portion of their membership to moderate and liberal bodies. One-seventh of the present liberals and one-fifth of the present moderates indicated that their most recent previous denomination was conservative.

When the data are analyzed according to regions of the country and by rural or urban location, we find: *a*) the liberals have gained measurably in Southern small towns and rural areas (+16 per cent), have grown slightly in Northern urban (+3 per cent) and Northern small towns and rural areas (+4 per cent), while declining slightly in Southern urban areas (—3 per cent); *b*) moderate denominations have gained in urban areas both North (+5 per cent) and South (+15 per cent), while losing slightly in the small towns and rural areas of the North; *c*) with the exception of a 7 per cent growth in Northern small towns and rural areas, the conservative groups have lost members in both Northern and Southern urban areas (—17 per cent and —3 per cent, respectively) as well as in Southern small towns and rural areas (—2 per cent).

But if, then, the more liberal denominations are gaining and the conservatives are losing, why does it seem to virtually every observer of the American religious scene—be he sociologist, journalist, or theologian—that the conservatives are gaining? And why has the relative success of the moderates and liberals been reflected neither in their denominational membership statistics nor in the financial support which they are currently receiving? Ignoring for the moment the possibility that the observers are merely echoing one another, we may account for their verdict by distinguishing between conservative *growth* and conservative *influence*. There is no question that the sects and the Baptists are winning "people who are simply outside most of society's institutions, the isolated, often itinerant, extremely impoverished underdogs," persons with an intrinsic belief in religion.[30] Glock and Stark envision the following cycle: Although virtually all Americans claim a denominational "preference," only about half actually belong to a specific local congregation. Persons who move into the middle classes tend to have prior family ties with or personal preference for the more conservative bodies. Such persons also tend to mark their passage into middle-class existence by joining a local congregation. It is highly probable that they will join a conservative church group. Hence, Glock and Stark maintain, "in terms of members of actual congregations, rather than mere denominational acknowledgment, the conservative ranks may be filling from newly affluent lower-class persons." [31] But as previous members of conservative bodies become established members of the middle class, they move on to more moderate and liberal bodies. In addition, these groups are joined by persons who have previously remained outside the church, *e.g.* middle- and upper-class individuals raised by parents who rejected church affiliation out of personal conviction. In the meantime, the ranks of the more liberal congregations are depleted as middle- and upper-class persons drop out of the churches altogether due to the inability of such denominations to generate member commitment.

As we related in the previous chapter, the conservative churches are highly effective in eliciting the ritual, devotional, and financial support of their members. Conservative theological convictions regarding God, Jesus, the Bible, and salvation sound so proper to the majority of Americans that they claim them as their own. Conservative congregations are primary groups, focal points in the personal development and communal activities of their members; while liberal congregations evoke a much lower degree of loyalty or personal involvement. Again in the words of Glock and Stark, "the liberal congregations resemble theater audiences, their members are mainly strangers to one another." [32]

In sum, the conservative churches are both growing and declining at a rapid rate. But the relatively high degree of religious dedication shown by their members and the certainty of their convictions—convictions shared by the majority of Americans—enable them to exert considerable influence on American religion and American life as a whole at a time when the influence of the mainline denominations is waning. If fundamentalism appears to be on the march, the speed of its advance may seem much faster than it really is due to the present immobility of denominational and ecumenical Protestantism. Whether or not the doctrines of fundamentalism are suited to the needs of twentieth-century man, the conservatives are showing ardor, zeal, and dedication at a time when these qualities are generally absent from American life.

THE POLITICAL INFLUENCE OF AMERICAN RELIGION

What are the political implications of the religious beliefs and practices of the American population?

In a study of twenty bond issue referendums held in major cities between 1956 and 1963, James Q. Wilson and Edward C. Banfield found that low-income groups (Poles, Czechs, Italians, Irish, and other Catholic ethnic groups) offered the most opposition to bond issues for hospitals, recreational and school facilities despite the fact that they would pay the least for these and receive the greatest benefits. At the same time, upper-income white Protestant and Jewish voters, who pay the most and benefit the least from such expenditures, were the strongest supporters. Only one group responded to the referendums according to "rational self-interest"—and that group was low-income blacks.[33]

Michael Parenti contends that such "instances of political behavior which bear no rational relationship to maximizing a group's material and social self-interest" are influenced in large measure by religious beliefs as well as by socioeconomic interests.[34] Political predispositions, Parenti maintains, are shaped by beliefs concerning revealed dogma, salvation, the control of impulse, the value of reason, and the nature of evil. In support of his thesis, Parenti cites the contrast between Jewish liberalism and Catholic conservatism. As Wesley and Beverly Allinsmith observed nearly a quarter of a century ago, Jews rank with Presbyterians and Congregationalists in their socioeconomic level and white-collar status; yet their attitudes regarding job security are more like those of Baptist and Catholic workers.[35] This behavior might be explained as an outgrowth of the marginal social status of the Jews throughout much of their history; to say nothing of the unofficial but persistent anti-Semitism of the WASP Establishment.[36] Perhaps the fear that their present economic security is threatened by forces over which they have historically had no control influences the Jews to align themselves with a political philosophy which is of greater benefit to lower socioeconomic groups than to themselves. But, as Parenti states: Catholic ethnic groups such as the Poles, Irish, and Italians have repeatedly experienced military conquest, oppression, exploitation, and starvation. Their early immigrant days in the United States were no easier than those of the Jews; the prejudice and discrimination which they faced were not easily overcome. Yet the "liberal reform-mindedness" which is so characteristic of the Jewish community in America is almost entirely absent from the Catholic ethnic groups.[37]

If oppression and marginality have been the common lot of many groups, are there any factors in their religious heritage which might account for Jewish liberalism? Parenti concentrates on three: (*1*) a respect for intellectualism (and a lack of anti-intellectualism); (*2*) a this-worldly, ethical orientation; and (*3*) a rejection of asceticism. He notes that the "usual tension between faith and intellect does not grip Judaism." There is an intimate connection between learning and religion, a regard for human reason as well as for piety. The intellectual has never been an object of derision, but "a man to be esteemed and entrusted with the responsibilities of leadership and power." [38]

Because Judaism is less a system of beliefs and rituals than a code of practices and moral commitments, an essential part of Jewish identity is dedication to social betterment and justice. Personal piety alone does not make one a Jew. For redemption is found in partnership with God in the restoration of the creation to oneness—an indivisible living wholeness which manifests itself in the unity of God with his creation, the harmony of man with his fellows, the peace which restores and heals the individual.[39]

Because the creation is good, and man shares with God in its day-by-day perfecting, Judaism does not encourage ascetic renunciation as a means of personal salvation. As Parenti states, "A high value is placed on life in this world. Bodily appetites are understood to be natural and acceptable rather than sinful, and one does not face the world in a chronic state of antagonistic, guilt-ridden self-denial. . . . Life is reaffirmed rather than renounced."[40] As a result, the Jew is able to support liberal reforms intended to maximize man's happiness and well-being on earth without a sense of sin, worldliness, or hubris.

In comparison to the Jewish record of liberal-reformism, the Catholic response must be characterized as conservative. Although Catholics have tended to support the Democratic party, their enthusiasm for Father Coughlin and Senator Joseph McCarthy as well as their lukewarm response to civil rights and their support of reactionary causes and candidates in recent years give evidence of "an ultra-conservatism at least as virulent as any found among middle-class urban Protestants. . . ." It should be noted that Catholic attachment to the Democratic party decreases as income increases. In 1956 the Catholic vote actually went to the Republican party. John Kennedy regained this vote in 1960. In the 1968 election, a sizable portion of the Catholic vote went to third-party candidate George Wallace. At least a partial explanation is afforded by the sharp contrast between Catholic and Jewish orientation in each of the value areas under discussion. According to Parenti, Catholicism is (*1*) strongly anti-intellectual; (*2*) essentially individualistic in its conception of salvation; and (*3*) puritanic in its attitude toward earthly pleasures.[41]

The Roman Catholics interviewed by Glock and Stark resembled the conservative Protestants in some respects, the moderates in others, the liberals in still others, and none of the Protestants in a few. They would rank with the *conservatives* in the following matters: their conviction that God exists, their belief in the divinity of Jesus, their belief that there is a devil, their over-all orthodoxy and certainty as measured by the Glock-Stark indices, the regularity of their church attendance, the percentage of both affluent and poor members, their degree of devotionalism, their experiences of having been punished by God for previous sins, and the percentage which have no close friends among members of the local church.

The Catholics were also like the *liberal* Protestants in some ways: they were not particularly convinced that belief in Jesus as savior is essential, nor that being ignorant of Jesus or being Jewish could prevent salvation. Only one-quarter of the Catholics reported Christian salvation experiences; and 18 per cent had no religious experiences. The Catholics were even less religiously knowledgeable than the liberal Protestants. In fact, the Jewish respondents in the 1954 Gallup poll of religious knowledge were better informed than the Catholics as to the founders of religions other than their own, the names of major Old Testament prophets, the identity of the nation which ruled Jerusalem during the time of Jesus, and the identity of the author of the most books in the New Testament.

In the following respects, the Roman Catholics closely resembled the *moderate* Protestants. Only 47 per cent are convinced that Jesus will actually return to earth; 46 per cent scored high on the Glock-Stark ritual commitment index; only 43 per cent have experienced the presence of God; 36 per cent have felt tempted; and 57 per cent rated high on the religious experience index. Finally, 36 per cent of the Catholics report that three to five of their closest friends are members of their churches.

A religious system which stresses the immutability and purity of its dogma and the need for unquestioning obedience to its teachings is prone to distrust human reason and learning. Modern knowledge is looked upon not as categories in which the faith may be reformulated but as a threat to its sanctity. Parochial schools are not so much a place where learning and piety are joined as a sanctuary against heresy, secularity, and licentiousness. Such distrust of human reason is hardly compatible with programs which seek to ameliorate social ills.

The essential individualism of the Catholic faith directs energies toward personal salvation rather than social change. Further, concern for present conditions is seen as distracting one from his true religious responsibility—the saving of his eternal soul. Not only does Catholicism emphasize a personal rather than a communal concept of redemption, but it defines sin in equally individualistic terms. Sin is an isolated single act of disobedience. A good person is one who refrains from such acts or anything which might occasion them. The psychological superficiality of such an understanding of the human predicament manifests itself in Catholic reliance on individual initiative and disparagement of concerted action for the solution of social and economic problems. Again, the ideological basis for liberal-reformist activity is undercut.

While the Catholic church is not as ascetic as many fundamentalist sects, it does contain within it a definite antagonism toward the erotic and pleasurable aspects of human life. This ascetic tendency is operative in the Catholic emphasis upon the inherent sinfulness of human nature, the need to guard against fleshly temptation, the threat of eternal punishment for sins, and the need for constant constraint and discipline. "Evil is willed and individually, rather than socially caused." It is the consequence of "too much freedom." [42] Viewed from this perspective, the liberal's conviction that man may perfect himself without divine intervention is an invitation to license, lust, and self-indulgence. Because the liberal does not realize the radical sinfulness of human nature, he rationalizes away the evil-doer's responsibility for his own acts and encourages lawlessness. If he were aware that this world is only a "vale of soul-making," [43] he would dedicate his efforts not to eradicating the unhappiness of this world but in preparing for the happiness of the next.

But what of American Protestants? How would they be graded according to Parenti's criteria: (*1*) the relationship of faith and reason; (*2*) ethical orientation (this-worldliness versus other-worldliness; individualism versus communality); and (*3*) attitude toward natural pleasures (enjoyment versus asceticism). The same variety of responses which characterizes Protestantism on all matters of faith and life will be found in these areas. But, in general, the further to the right we move in the liberal-orthodox scale of Protestant groups utilized by Glock and Stark, the more nearly do we discover the Catholic-orthodox viewpoint described by Parenti. Thus, Congregationalists, Methodists, and Episcopalians will be rational, this-worldly, socially and politically action-minded, and non-ascetic in comparison to the anti-intellectual, other-worldly, individualistic, and ascetic conservatives (Missouri Lutherans, Southern Baptists, and members of Sects).

Parenti observes that although conservative Protestants reject the hierarchical control, priestly sacramentalism, elaborate ritual, and doctrinal traditionalism of the Catholic church; they do share with the Catholics a strong distrust of human reason, the acceptance of fixed and final dogmas, an other-worldly and individualistic concept of salvation, and an ascetic rejection of pleasure and secularity. For the conservative, the Bible is the inspired Word of God and the source of all wisdom. The truths of Scripture are revealed, fixed, and final. They are to be memorized and obeyed, not endlessly pondered and disputed. Human reason was corrupted by the Fall—the first man's rebellion against the Word of God. Intellectual inquiry can only lead one astray. In the words of Billy Graham:

> Nothing is gained psychologically or spiritually by casting aspersion on the Bible. A generation that occupied itself with criticism of the Scriptures all too soon found itself questioning divine revelation.[44]

As we have seen, the conservative Protestant considers the world lost in its irremediable wickedness. Only the Second Coming of Christ can rescue mankind from its boundless perversity. Parenti notes, "Man is guilty of hubris in thinking that he can solve the world's ills through secular effort." God alone can overcome the sinfulness of the human heart. The conservative is more interested in avoiding temptation than in resisting injustice. From his perspective the church is not an agency for the improvement of the world; it is an ark in which to escape from its irreversible evil.

But does the conservative Protestant's condemnation of human striving mean that theological and political conservatism are inseparable? In 1968 Milton Rokeach examined the relation between the religious beliefs and social compassion of over 1,000 adult Americans ranging in age from 21 to 80. He found that "those who place a high value on salvation are conservative, anxious to maintain the *status quo* and unsympathetic to the black and the poor." Many of them reacted gleefully to the news of the assassination of Martin Luther King, Jr., were unsympathetic with student protests, and felt that the church should not become involved in social or political issues. Rokeach concludes:

> Considered all together the data suggest a portrait of the religious-minded as a churchgoer who has a self-centered preoccupation with saving his own soul, and an alienated, otherworldly orientation coupled with indifference toward—a tacit endorsement of—a social system that would perpetuate social inequality and injustice.[45]

The church, he adds, has done a much better job of instructing Americans what *not* to do than what they *ought* to do. Richard V. Pierard, a conservative Protestant, maintains, "The ties linking evangelical Christianity to political conservatism are so numerous and pervasive that it is possible to say the two are 'yoked together.' "[46] He complains that by its support of the political right, the conservative theological position has "tied itself to the *status quo* of contemporary middle-class America and traded its prophetic ministry for a pottage of public acclaim and economic well-being."[47] But it seems clear that conservative Protestantism in general has no more converted to the radical right than liberal Protestantism has to the radical left. A few separatists such as Carl McIntire and Billy James Hargis have found their following among reactionary political elements, but the vast majority of Middle Americans scarcely sympathize with the amalgamation of conservative biblicism, laissez-faire capitalism, anti-Communist paranoia, racial discrimination, uncompromising jingoism, and absolute opposition to social welfare legislation peculiar to such ultra-fundamentalists. Not only are the ultra-fundamentalists unrepresentative of conservative Protestantism as a whole, but they are woefully out of touch with the sentiments of the emerging political majority. Middle America's faith is neither the reactionary ultra-fundamentalism of the hatemongers nor the well-meaning liberalism of the East Coast urban establishment. The faith of Middle America is a combination of two ideologically disparate elements: fundamentalism and America's civil religion. In addition it is constantly affected by America's liberal-humanist heritage. The liberal-humanist heritage exists in many manifestations apart from the civil religion; but the civil religion is inconceivable without the progressivism, rationalism, and internationalism of the liberal spirit. Thus, when we speak of faith in the American Way of Life, we are speaking of a civil religion which borrows symbols and substance from both the Bible and American liberalism. It is to a consideration of America's civil religion that we now turn our attention.

NOTES

1. Will Herberg, *Protestant-Catholic-Jew* (Garden City: Doubleday, 1955), p. 81.
2. T. B. Bottomore, *Class in Modern Society* (New York: Vintage Books, 1966), pp. 29–30; 85–87; John H. Goldthorpe and David Lockwood, "Affluence and the British Class Structure," *The Sociological Review*, XI, 2 (July, 1963), pp. 133–63.
3. Herberg, *op. cit.*, p. 80.

4. *American Piety: The Nature of Religious Commitment,* Vol. 1, Patterns of Religious Commitment (Berkeley and Los Angeles: University of California Press, 1968), p. 98.
5. Stuart E. Rosenberg, in *What Do We Believe? The Stance of Religion in America* (New York: Meredith Press, 1968), p. 53.
6. The results of the Glock-Stark surveys are found in *American Piety: The Nature of Religious Commitment* and *Christian Beliefs and Anti-Semitism* (New York: Harper and Row, 1966).
7. New York *Times,* November 28, 1971, p. 48.
8. *American Piety, op. cit.,* p. 104.
9. *Christianity Today,* March 31, 1958, reprinted in *A Christianity Today Reader,* edited by Frank E. Gaebelein (New York: Meredith Press, 1966), pp. 12–14.
10. *American Piety, op. cit.,* p. 75.
11. Study No. 539-K, *ibid.,* pp. 161–162.
12. Percentage of members with annual incomes of $10,000 or more: Missouri Lutheran, 41; Southern Baptist, 26; Sects, 22. Percentage with incomes of $6,000 or less: Missouri Lutheran, 23; Southern Baptist, 31; Sects, 43. According to both statistics, Missouri Lutherans are almost identical in economical status to the Episcopalians and all the moderate denominations.
13. Bernard S. Phillips, *Sociology: Social Structure and Change* (New York: The Macmillan Company, 1969), p. 101. *Cf.* Charles H. Cooley, *Social Organization* (New York: The Free Press, 1956).
14. The current growth rate of the Southern Baptist Convention (1.7 per cent a year) exceeds the growth rate of the national population (1.3 per cent). Edwin S. Gaustad, "America's Institutions of Faith," in *Religion in America,* edited by William G. McLoughlin and Robert N. Bellah (Boston: Houghton Mifflin Company, 1968), p. 114.
15. *What Do We Believe?, op. cit.,* p. 299.
16. "Contemporary Religious Appeals and Who Responds," *Religion and the Face of America,* Papers presented at Asilomar, Pacific Grove, Calif., November 28–30, 1958 (Berkeley, Calif.: University Extension, University of California, 1959), p. 9.
17. "Is There a Third Force in Christendom?" *Religion in America, op. cit.,* p. 45.
18. The contributions received by radio evangelists Oral Roberts, Rex Humbard, and Carl McIntire which enabled them to obtain the real estate for these three schools are fantastic. Eight-year-old Oral Roberts University in Tulsa, Okla., is a coeducational, privately controlled liberal arts institution with 1,033 students and 87 faculty members. Rex Humbard bought the $17 million campus of defunct Mackinac College for $3 million in April, 1971. In a recent interview, McIntire claimed that his organization held control of $25 million of holdings in the vicinity of the Cape, including the Cape Kennedy Hilton, the convention center, the IBM building, and the Boeing building. (Other sources in the area of the Cape say that McIntire has been unable to take legal title to these holdings due to inadequate financing.) Organizations controlled by McIntire also own the Christian Admiral Hotel in Cape May, N.J., Shelton College in the same city (which, for failure to meet accreditation standards, has been deprived of its degree-granting privileges by the state of New Jersey), and Faith Theological Seminary in Elkins Park, Penna.

19. Rasmussen, in Proceedings of a Conference on Religion and Society, held and published by The University of California Press, Berkeley.
20. *Ibid.*, pp. 14–15.
21. Robert Coles, *The Middle Americans* (Boston: Little, Brown and Company, 1971), p. 132.
22. *Ibid.*, pp. 10–11.
23. In the fifties editors of major publishing houses maintained that fundamentalists read nothing but the Bible. Hence, it would be foolish to publish books aimed at them. Today, one hears that liberal Protestants are so interested in sociology, black studies, the New Left, ecology *et al,* that there is no reason to publish *religious* books directed to them.
24. Among the many excellent critiques of education in America, the following is particularly noteworthy: John Holt, *How Children Fail* (New York: Delta Books, 1964).
25. Abraham Kaplan, *American Ethics and Public Policy* (New York: Oxford University Press, 1963), p. 49.
26. See Chapter 1, pp. 13–21.
27. "The Protestant Churches," *The Annals of the American Academy of Political and Social Science,* Vol. 256, March 1948, p. 50.
28. *American Piety, op. cit.*, p. 201.
29. Edwin S. Gaustad, in *Religion in America, op. cit.*, p. 127.
30. *American Piety, op. cit.*, p. 202.
31. *Ibid.*
32. *Ibid.*, p. 221.
33. James Q. Wilson and Edward C. Banfield, "Public Regardingness As a Value Premise in Voting Behavior," *American Political Science Review,* 58 (1964), pp. 876–887.
34. Michael Parenti, "Political Values and Religious Cultures: Jews, Catholics, and Protestants," *Journal for the Scientific Study of Religion,* Fall 1967, pp. 259–269.
35. "Religious Affiliation and Politico-Economic Attitude," *Public Opinion Quarterly,* XII (1948), pp. 377–389.
36. See E. Digby Baltzell, *The Protestant Establishment, Aristocracy and Caste in America* (New York: Random House, 1964).
37. Michael Parenti, *op. cit.*, pp. 261–262.
38. *Ibid.*
39. See Lowell D. Streiker, *The Promise of Buber* (New York: J. B. Lippincott Company, 1969), pp. 19–28.
40. Michael Parenti, *op. cit.*, p. 263.
41. *Ibid.*, pp. 264–265.
42. *Ibid.*, p. 265.
43. *Ibid.*
44. Billy Graham, "Biblical Authority in Evangelism," in *A Christianity Today Reader, op. cit.*, pp. 22–23.
45. Milton Rokeach, "Faith, Hope and Bigotry," *Psychology Today,* April 1970, p. 58.
46. Richard V. Pierard, *The Unequal Yoke, Evangelical Christianity and Political Conservatism* (Philadelphia: J. B. Lippincott Company, 1970), p. 18. *Cf.* Jorstad, *The Politics of Doomsday.*
47. *Ibid.*

5

The Religion of Middle America

Since the early years of the Republic, foreign observers of the American scene have been struck by the high degree of religious involvement as well as by the superficiality of our religious commitments. Religion has been firmly entrenched in American society since the beginning. And whatever the fate of institutionalized religion in other parts of the world, our present church membership figures suggest that the influence of religion upon the American Way of Life is as strong as ever. We may suspect the depth, sophistication, and consistency of American religion, but it is difficult to deny the abiding religiosity of the American people.

In contrast, religion in Europe has been on the decline for many years. Church membership, along with participation in church-sponsored activities, has steadily shrunk as the social base of the churches has dwindled. Having lost urban dwellers and industrial workers, the churches have been restricted "to that part of the population which is peripheral to the structure of modern society: the peasantry, the remnants of the traditional bourgeoisie and petite bourgeoisie within the middle classes, which are not . . . involved in the typical work processes of industrial urban society." [1]

Everywhere but in America, church religion has become a marginal phenomenon in modern society. The continuing vitality of American religion (at least in quantitative terms) belies the hypothesis that "secular man" can live without God. In Luckmann's words:

> The most "modern" of the countries under discussion, the United States, shows the highest degree of involvement in church religion. To compound the difficulties [of those who claim the progressive spread of secularization], the high American figures of overt participation represent, in all likelihood, a fairly recent upward movement rather than a decrease from a yet higher level.[2]

And yet, as Wilson asserts, "No one is prepared to suggest that America is other than a secularized country." Even though we cling to our churches for social identification, for comfort, for moral guidance; America is, "a country in which instrumental values, rational procedures and technical methods have gone furthest, and the country in which the sense of the sacred, the sense of the sanctity of life, and deep religiosity are most conspicuously absent."[3] The dominant values of American culture, we are told, are not religious.

THE CREED OF MIDDLE AMERICA

Despite our high degree of participation in church activities and the relative orthodoxy of our theological convictions, Americans are motivated by what Herberg describes as:

> Some sort of faith or belief or set of convictions, not generally designated as religion but definitely operative as such in [our] lives in the sense of providing . . . some fundamental context of normality and meaning.[4]

Indeed, the power of this implicit faith is so great that the nominal fundamentalism which Americans profess is prevented under ordinary circumstances from becoming the primary source of their socio-political motivations. The content of this common religion, according to Herberg, is an implicit faith in "the American Way of Life." We are as a people bound together by a limited number of fundamental affirmations which transcend the claims of all other beliefs in dignity and power. The principal ingredients are: "individual freedom, personal independence, human dignity, community responsibility, social and political democracy, sincerity, restraint in outward conduct, thrift, . . . the uniqueness of the American 'order,' and the great importance assigned to religion." [5]

The socio-political attitudes of Americans are influenced by what they believe to be ultimately true, real, and desirable. One source of such convictions is the religion of their churches. A second source is civil religion, the implicit faith in the American Way of Life. This source borrows its symbols and its substance from pietistic Christianity as well as liberal-humanism. The convictions of the American liberal tradition are as follows: man is a rational being capable of solving the problems of his society through the application of reason and technology; the United States of America is based on self-evident truths (embodied in the Declaration of Independence, the Constitution, and its various institutions); and the special destiny of America is to spread these truths to all the nations of the world and to remove all obstructions to the realization of these truths. The liberal-humanist heritage in no way depends upon the civil religion. But there could be no American civil religion without the liberal tradition.

Alongside the creeds of the churches we attend, Americans possess a more basic set of precepts: the belief in skill, competence, efficiency, perseverance, and organization; the willingness to respond to competition; and the conviction that the United States enjoys a special destiny in the world.[6] As Herberg elaborates:

> If the American Way of Life had to be defined in one word, "democracy" would undoubtedly be the word, but democracy in a peculiarly American sense. On its political side it means the Constitution; on its economic side, "free enterprise"; on its social side, an equalitarianism which is not only compatible with but indeed actually implies vigorous economic competition and high mobility. . . .
>
> The American Way of Life is individualistic, dynamic, prag-

> matic. It affirms the supreme value and dignity of the individual; it stresses incessant activity on his part . . . ; it defines an ethic of self-reliance, merit, and character, and judges by achievement. . . . The American Way of Life is humanitarian, "forward looking," optimistic. . . . The American believes in progress, in self-improvement, and quite fanatically in education. But above all, the American is idealistic. . . . And because they are so idealistic, Americans tend to be moralistic: they are inclined to see all issues as plain and simple, black and white, issues of morality.[7]

Our culture is marked, we are told, "by a central stress upon personal achievement, especially secular occupational achievement. The 'success story' and the respect accorded to the self-made man are distinctly American. . . ." [8] Did not William James chide us a half century ago for "our national disease . . . , the worship of the bitch-goddess SUCCESS"? [9]

We are bound to the creed of Middle America, to belief in the American Way of Life. We see ourselves as the "New Order of the Ages," the beginning of a unique and superior society ordained and protected by God. Religious institutions have an important role to play in the promulgation of this American Way of Life, for they sanctify the aims, ideals, and standards of the implicit common faith. And because the churches proclaim, defend, apply, and legitimate the American Way of Life—because the churches are the first and most vehement accusers of all who deviate from the implicit faith—Americans grant to religion a place of honor and dignity shared by no other social institution. To put it simply, Americans believe in religion. As Miller observes: "The faith [of Americans] is not in God but in faith; we worship not God but our own worshipping." [10]

AMERICA'S CIVIL RELIGION

But belief in the American Way of Life is not the sum and substance of our common religion. We see *this* particular style of life as desirable, experience *this* set of demands as binding, seek fulfillment through *these* promises because of an even more fundamental relationship to reality. Religion is more than affirmation about "right" and "wrong" or the pursuit of the good life. A man's religion is his relationship with that which he regards as central in the nature of things, that which is both indubitable and inescapable. And this relationship shapes his thoughts, his feelings, his actions, and the society in which he lives. Religion is an individual's response to that which he experiences as ultimate, as most valuable, as dearest to himself, as most real and intense. Religion is a dynamic living with the gap between the way things ought to be and the way they are.

Every society has a "religious dimension," a fundamental response to reality which gives it a sense of what ought to be, its understanding of its national experience in the light of ultimate reality. The basis of the common religion of the American Way of Life is what Robert N. Bellah has termed "an elaborate and well-institutionalized civil religion in America, . . . a religious dimension . . . [which] has its own seriousness and integrity and requires the same care in understanding that any religion does." [11] Robert E. Osgood discerns the formative influence of such intrinsic ultimate values at work in American foreign policy:

> Unless Americans constantly relate their pursuit of national security and national interest to a hierarchy of universal values, they will, ultimately, drive out of their national, as well as their international conduct, those moral qualities which are as indispensable to national welfare as character is to personal welfare. . . . If the . . . values which are the basis for America's social and political institutions are valid at all, they are as valid outside American borders as within.[12]

There is an *American* response to ultimate reality which is the source of the vision of what-ought-to-be embracing the life of each American, his society, and the world in which he lives. It is the wellspring of religious and moral values which determine our self-understanding and sense of national vocation. The American religion is colored by the Bible; it expresses itself in biblical archetypes: "Exodus, Chosen People, Promised Land, New Jerusalem, Sacrificial Death and Rebirth." [13] But it interprets each of these concepts in the light of a religious experience which is "genuinely American and genuinely new." American civil religion "has its own prophets and its own martyrs, its own sacred events and sacred places, its own solemn rituals and symbols." [14] American civil religion is not the worship of the American nation, but a frame of reference for the understanding and valuation of American experience.

The dogmas of civil religion are simple: "the existence of God, the life to come, the reward of virtue and the punishment of vice, and the exclusion of religious intolerance." [15] The God of the founding fathers and statesmen of the early Republic is clearly not the "God and Father of our Lord Jesus Christ." He is "much more related to order, law, and right than to salvation and love." [16] But neither is he the Deist's absentee worldmaker. The God of the civil religion is "actively interested and involved in history, with a special concern for America." America is seen as the new Israel, the promised land. Declares Bellah:

> Until the Civil War, the American civil religion focused above all on the event of the Revolution, which was seen as the final act of the Exodus from the old lands across the waters. The Declaration of Independence and the Constitution were the sacred scriptures and Washington the divinely appointed Moses who led his people out of the hands of tryranny.[17]

The horror and chaos of the Civil War evoked a new search for national meaning, and greatly deepened the symbolism of the civic religion. The bloodiest war in American history (in terms of percentage of the entire population killed, wounded, or otherwise directly affected) added the themes of death, sacrifice, and rebirth to the civil religion. A "new testament" was introduced into our national consciousness by Abraham Lincoln. "For us and our country," remarks Robert Lowell, "he left Jefferson's ideals of freedom and equality joined to the Christian sacrificial act of death and rebirth." A man might die, many men would die, in the War Between the States. But, according to Lincoln, their deaths would not be in vain. For "this nation, under God, shall have a new birth of freedom. . . ." Sacrifice and death so that the nation might be renewed—such was the message and the heroic example of our first martyred President.

Like all *American* religion, the civil religion is highly pietistic: zealous, enthusiastic, emotional, individualistic, and messianic. As William G. McLoughlin discerns:

> To be an American is to belong to a pietistic sect. . . . Sometimes the mission expresses itself in terms of an example to the world—as in the case of the Bible Commonwealth of the Puritan city upon a hill or the new nation of 1776 dedicated to certain inalienable rights of man; sometimes it expresses itself in more aggressive forms as "manifest destiny" or "the white man's burden" to bring democracy and Christianity to the heathen or "the undeveloped"; sometimes it makes war to end colonialism (1898), to make the world safe for democracy (1917), or to prevent the immoral aggression of atheistic, totalitarian Communism (today); sometimes it dedicates its most idealistic young men to missionary endeavor and to Peace Corps evangelism; and sometimes it simply gives away its "filthy lucre" to help the poor, the weak, and the unfortunate, as in the Marshall Plan, Point Four, the Alliance for Progress, and foreign aid in general. Despite all the charges of self-interest, pragmatism, or hypocrisy that can be leveled at these actions, European observers have generally recognized that the United States is unique among nations because it professes to a conscience as well as a mission.[18]

"To be an American is to belong to a pietistic sect," that is the key phrase to understanding the relation of the faith of Billy Graham to the American civil religion. Although revivalistic Protestantism and the creed of Middle America provide two distinctly different sets of symbols, they readily combine as sources of individual motivation and social morality. An individual's religion is his experience of, response and

commitment to, Ultimate Reality in his specific socio-historical context. It is his relationship to whatever he regards as of "ultimate importance in his own life, and as having to do with what he regards as permanent or central in the nature of things." [19] Religion is a dynamic living with the gap between the way things ought to be and the way they are, between one's vision of the eternal and his apprehension of present realities.

The religion of a mature individual is what psychologists term a "master sentiment"—that is, an organized motive or disposition developed through experience to respond favorably and habitually to those conceptual objects and principles which are of greatest importance to the individual and which he considers ultimate, unconditional, and absolute in the greater scheme of things. Our research suggests that Americans respond favorably and habitually to principles drawn from at least three diverse sources: the Christianity of America's revivalistic heritage (a heritage currently exemplified in the message of Billy Graham); an optimistic and messianic commitment to the "American Way of Life" (a faith which manifests itself in "Honor America Day" and the official utterances of virtually every public officeholder); and a progressive, rationalistic spirit of dedication to the solution of social problems through manipulation of social structures (which is usually designated "liberalism").

Actively or reactively the civil religion has been borrowing its substance from both revivalism and liberalism. Sometimes the revivalistic heritage possessed greater evocative power (consider the text of "The Battle Hymn of the Republic" and Lincoln's "Gettysburg Address"). At other times the liberal's evolutionary modernism reigned supreme (remember our celebrations of "the secular city"?). Most of the time, there are subtle tensions (and often not-so-subtle tensions) between the two traditions—even though the civil religion continues to draw upon both.

Although the American civil religion does not claim the exclusive devotion of its adherents, it does have its own distinct rituals and forms. Memorial Day, which integrates local communities into the civic cult, and Thanksgiving Day, which assimilates the family into the national religion, provide an annual ritual calendar. At its worst, the civil religion "has suffered various deformations and demonic distortions." At its best, it has consistently represented a higher level of moral consciousness than the churches. The principal distortions have been the use of the American Israel theme as justification for the destruction of our Indian population and a pretense for our various imperialistic adventures. Bellah admits that our civil religion "has often been used and is being used today as a cloak for petty interests and ugly passions. . . . It is in need—as is any living faith—of continual reform, of being measured by universal standards. But it is not evident that it is incapable of growth and new insight." [20] Nor is it impossible that such a religion could outlive the Christian churches of America. For the evocative power of the symbols of the American civil religion is in no way dependent upon Christianity. Their efficacy derives from the history of the American people and the universality of their relevance. For the faith that freedom and equality may be attained through sacrifice and dedication is not limited to Americans. American institutions could survive the decline or disappearance of the religion of the churches, but the decline of faith in American civil religion would surely mean the end of all that we value. For without the personal motivation and national purpose provided by our faith in America's special destiny as guardian of liberty, the American Way of Life can be supported only by greed and coercion.

SIGNIFICANCE OF THE WHITE HOUSE RELIGIOUS SERVICES

Richard M. Nixon has done more than any previous President to create a syncretism of church religion and civil religion through the institution of White House religious services. Edward B. Fiske, religion editor of the New York *Times*, says:

> Conceived of by Richard M. Nixon shortly before his inauguration in 1969, the White House church services have become something of a new national ritual, part of the fabric of the Nixon Administration and, inevitably, of the nation's religious life. They have been attacked as a threat to separation of church and state, and lamented as mindless expressions of a religion that has become indistinguishable from prevailing cultural values. . . . But defenders of the services, which are convened once a month or so, cite them as evidence of the country's continuing recognition of its spiritual foundations.[21]

The preachers are personally selected by the President. The "worshippers" receive official invitations from the White House social secretary, Lucy Winchester. The liturgy is a "common denominator" service intended to accommodate all participants. Fiske reports:

> Worshippers at the White House . . . are more of an audience than a congregation. They do not even join in the singing of hymns. The liturgical casualness of the rites was probably most evident on two occasions when rabbis who were asked to lead the service stood by while the rest of the assemblage sang the Doxology in praise of the Christian Trinity.[22]

The late Reinhold Niebuhr characterized the White House services as the establishment of "a conforming religion." It is remarkable, he said, "what a simple White House invitation will do to dull the critical faculties, thereby confirming the worst fears of the Founding Fathers." [23] But Will Herberg has observed that the President has provided a solid institutional form for the "free-floating piety" loosed by the breakdown of traditional religious allegiances. As Charles P. Henderson, Jr., remarks, the public utterances of President Nixon reveal that he is a "theologican" of American civil religion. "Nixon appropriates the vocabulary of theologians—faith, hope, belief—and applies these words not to a transcendent God but to his own nation." The President, maintains Henderson, "has made patriotism his religion, the American dream his deity."[24] Henderson, Fiske, and Garry Wills have all criticized the President for his "lack of a sense of transcendence." But the America of American civil religion is scarcely less "transcendent" than is the God of the Judeo-Christian tradition.

Richard M. Nixon's religious heritage is strictly evangelical. The particular Quaker sect in which Nixon was reared has been described as fundamentalist in theology, emotional, and revivalistic. As a youth, Nixon went forward to make a "decision for Christ" at an evangelistic rally.[25] No matter how much the President may have reduced religion to ethics and the support of national policy, it is not hard to detect the evangelical fervor of his civil faith. Could we conceive of any other national statesman appearing at a Billy Graham evangelistic rally—as the President did in 1970 on the campus of the University of Tennessee? We may have wondered about Billy Graham's association with previous Presidents. What did he discuss with Harry Truman, General Eisenhower, or JFK? But the association of the man who has led millions to Christ and of the President who believes in his country seems natural. For both are manifestations of America's residual pietism. According to Fiske:

> The success of Mr. Nixon's homely style is proven by the thousands of requests that flow in from people who want to touch the hem of East Room religion. "It's the most popular thing we have," Lucy Winchester declares. "Americans are basically religious, and this seems to speak to a fundamental American ethic. People don't identify very well with state dinners, but they are familiar with prayer. The honor of being able to pray with the President is something that they regard as special."
>
> And so they come on an average of once a month, not the poor and oppressed or the minorities . . . , but the powerful in Washington and a healthy sprinkling of the people who put Mr. Nixon in office, and they sit around him in worship of the Almighty. As the wife of the undertaker from Long Island put it, "It's nice to see so much of Middle America in one place."[26]

RELIGION AS DEFENDER OF THE STATUS QUO

Are we, then, a religious or a secular country? In truth we are both. For, from the very beginning of our national experience, we have located religion in the sphere of private preference. We believe that being religious is a good thing—regardless of the nature, history, traditions, dogmas, or ethical norms of the various specific religions which various citizens profess. We are a tolerant people, believing that all religions are equally good and none is altogether false. We maintain this tolerance—this distinctively American tolerance—even though it is diametrically opposed to the creed of virtually every religion which Americans profess. (This tolerance is, however, absolutely essential to our inherent civil religion).

Until quite recently we have been a nation of immigrants. Our ancestors suffered from the wars, persecutions, and prejudices occasioned by taking religion as seriously as religion claims it should be taken. Better superficiality and inconsistency, they insisted, than fanaticism and civil war. And the pluralistic experiment worked beyond their fondest hopes. The individual was granted freedom *of* religion; the state guaranteed freedom *from* religion. Church and state became partners in the task of nation-building. Religion sanctified our national purposes; encouraged hard work, thrift, family and civic responsibility; provided comfort and security in an impersonal and threatening mass society. The state accepted the authority of religion in the private sphere—for example, it recognized the churches' right to marry, bury, indoctrinate, and exhort; it exempted ministers from military service; freed church property from tax burdens; encouraged the private religiosity of its citizens by paying the salaries of military and congressional chaplains; affirmed its faith in faith (the inscription "In God we trust" on our money; the phrase "under God" in the Pledge of Allegiance); and recognized the importance and prestige of institutional religion in ways which range from the intercessory prayers at Presidential inaugurations to swearing oaths upon the Bible in courts of law.

As Wilson observes:

> Religious commitment and Church allegiance *have become* elements in the American value system, accepted parts of "the American way of life." . . . Religion has placed its common values at the service of the political and social institutions of the nation, and has become one of the various approved values of American culture.[27]

But the cost of placing its "common values" at the service of the nation in order to contribute a transcendental justification for the norms and values of the established order is the reduction of divergent religious creeds to their lowest common denominator. Creedal differences are glossed over, liturgical services and even church architecture become indistinguishable to the point of redundancy.

American religion has acted and is acting as a defender of the American *status quo*. It provides stability in a society which would otherwise be experienced as chaotic and disjoined. "For when the rate of social change accelerates beyond a given point, the ability to maintain a sense of connection with the past and future disappears. . . ." [28] As Calvin Redekop declares:

> America is being dominated and undergirded by a pecuniary philosophy and a pragmatic ethic. A society which tends to value experimentation and change may need to have an institution that tends to preserve the good and proven values, truths and practices. Religion has served this function in the past, and there is every reason to assume that the function is necessary in America as well. It is entirely possible that a society without a strong defender of the tested traditions could become increasingly unstable and ultimately be destroyed through a lack of an inner gyroscope. At least until a functional alternative is found, religion in America may well be a very significant force in the maintenance of a stable way of life.[29]

But if, as the critics of religion contend, the creeds and

symbols of the churches of America represent a universe of meaning which is totally irrelevant to the culture of modern urban industrial society, how can religion continue to act as our inner gyroscope? To this question there are two possible answers, each of which has its proponents in the churches of America. First, the churches may limit their attention to social groups which continue to be oriented toward the values of the past. In this way, the churches will identify themselves as guardians of the "faith of the Founding Fathers," *i.e.* as custodians of the beliefs and ethical values of a sentimentally imagined earlier America. Second, the churches may accommodate themselves to the culture of our present technological society, providing legitimacy for the demands of industry and government. And, of course, the churches may combine both approaches, furnishing individuals with solace and security by means of the celebration of romanticized virtues more appropriate to agrarian and small-town existence, and thus diverting their attention from the real problems of social life in the present.

Indispensability of the Work Ethic

Many times the tensions between the romantic and the secular approaches produce baffling dilemmas. For example, the churches' abiding dedication to an individualistic work ethic is cited by many as an obstacle to any solution of the problems caused by modern automation. Redekop accuses the churches of promoting the Protestant ethic "in a time when there is almost no demonstrable relationship between the old virtues attributed to work, and the function and availability of work." While the concept of a negative income tax and a guaranteed annual income are "receiving increasing acceptance as the only solution to the problem of automation and cybernation," he states, "the Church generally seems to evade the consequences and still preaches a Gospel of individual initiative and the virtue of work." [30]

But is the abandonment of the work ethic really desirable? Before we can answer, we must explore the origin and significance of the Protestant Ethic. Max Weber, to whom we are indebted for this important concept, sought to account for the affinity between Protestantism and the commercial spirit. He documented the manner in which certain types of Protestantism had provided incentives for the pursuit of economic gain during and after the Reformation.[31] He states:

> The people of that period had after all very specific ideas of what awaited them in the life after death, of the means by which they could improve their chances in this respect, and they adjusted their conduct in accordance with these ideas. The orientation of their conduct varied with the different ideas concerning the conditions which [the individual] must fulfill in order to be sure of his salvation. And these ideas became significant for the development of culture—however difficult it may be for modern man to visualize the power and the torment of those metaphysical conceptions.[32]

The Reformed tradition was inspired by Calvin's doctrine of predestination according to which each individual's state of grace was determined for all time by God's inexorable decree before the creation of the world. Each man stands alone. Nothing—neither priestly sacraments nor the Church nor the secular community—can help him attain grace. Either he is among the elect or he is not. Bendix explains:

> . . . one must find solace on the basis of true faith. Each man was duty-bound to consider himself chosen and to reject all doubt as a temptation of the devil, for a lack of self-confidence was interpreted as a sign of insufficient faith. To attain that self-confidence, unceasing work in a calling was recommended. By his unceasing activity in the service of God, the believer strengthened his self-confidence as the active tool of the divine will.[33]

Only an active life guided by constant thought and self-control could conquer the state of nature and offer proofs of election. The active, rational, disciplined life was praised by the Puritan divines as a defense against doubt and the temptations of the flesh. Time was seen as a precious resource which must not be wasted in vain amusement. Every minute must be used to serve the glory of God and demonstrate the election of the individual. Profit and wealth are not evil unless they are spent for frivolous pleasures. Indeed, material gain was viewed as God's gift which man should accept as further proof of election and as a stewardship for which he would be held accountable. Work is decreed by God, it is not an end unto itself, but a means of confirming the fate of the individual in the world to come.

Clearly, the Protestant Ethic provides capitalism with religious justification. Work, which in an agrarian society is life itself or a central portion of life, becomes a *calling* or a *vocation,* a means of serving God and attaining psychological assurance of one's eternal election. Work is seen as a religious and moral duty, and, at least in theory, material reward is displaced as a motivating factor. But what happens when the religious understanding of man and his destiny which undergirds the Protestant Ethic disappears? Work is no longer a calling; it is no longer valued as a religious commitment. Instead, work is a means to an end—to the amassing and enjoyment of material goods, the attainment of prestige, the acquisition of power, etc. What was formerly a *calling* performed with dedication becomes a *job* undertaken with scant enthusiasm for the sake of limited, concrete ends. As Wilson observes:

> The Protestant Ethic has been responsible for a high level of disinterested goodwill, of honesty and integrity in personal as well as social spheres. Whether or not we can any longer accept its theological presuppositions, we have all benefited from its motivating force. For its influence has kept the corruption, crime, nepotism of modern society within bounds. It has facilitated a pattern of very general socialization . . . in which a strongly internalized sense of impersonal individual honesty has been widely created.[34]

It has made it unnecessary for American society to rely on compulsion, surveillance, threats, or bribery as means of social control.

But with the passing of religious values upon which the Protestant Ethic rests and the decline of the influence of religious institutions upon public life, we now see patterns of delinquency and disorder. And such must be expected in an achievement-oriented society which legitimates work not in religious or ethical terms but in essentially hedonistic ones. It is doubtful that our society will be able to maintain public order without resort to organized coercion, should the religious supports to the work-ethic be removed.

Where should the churches stand on this issue? Should they declare that work is obsolete and advocate a welfare-supported contemplative life-style? Or should they resist the ongoing re-evaluation of work and the consequent restructuring of the economy by proclaiming the virtues of an earlier, simpler America—virtues which may be only of sentimental value today? One course may produce a relevant faith which contributes to the destruction of the American way; the other to a pietistic and irrelevant faith which stubbornly refuses to recognize the nature of the society in which it finds itself.

Lack of Confidence Can Kill a Civilization

But perhaps we are making the mistake of equating the *Protestant Ethic* and *Protestantism.* Perhaps the American work ethic has been operative from the beginning of our history without the transcendental or eschatological support of Christian doctrine. If this is the case, the decline of Protestantism or the failure of the churches to accommodate themselves to the present work-devaluing situation would in no way threaten the power of our work ethic. We would contend that the American work ethic derives from the American civil religion rather than from the theology of the New England Puritans. For centuries our open frontiers, our boundless opportunities, and the absence of the class and religious restrictions of European society were sufficient to lure men to the hard work of nation-building. Further, the emergence of a distinctive religious coloration, a national ideology which saw the new situation as a religious quest, has been powerfully evocative. Men willingly postponed immediate satisfactions to participate in the establishment of God's kingdom—America. The saints of the Republic—Washington, Jefferson, and Lincoln—provided strong exemplars for our imitation and moral-religious rhetoric overflowing with symbols for our self-understanding. More recently, the power of the symbols of our national faith was replenished by the idealism of Woodrow Wilson, Franklin D. Roosevelt, and John F. Kennedy; and perhaps even more by the tragic death of the young President and his brother.

But the civil religion is today in greater jeopardy than the religion of the churches. The uncertainty of the times, political and military involvements which have brought our nation so little glory and so much unrest, a rate of change which our national traditions have not been able to absorb—here is the real threat to our purposes and values as a people. Concluding his superb television series "Civilisation," Kenneth Clark declared:

> It is lack of confidence, more than anything else, that kills a civilisation. We can destroy ourselves by cynicism and disillusion, just as effectively as by bombs. Fifty years ago W. B. Yeats, who was more like a man of genius than anyone I have ever known, wrote a famous prophetic poem.
>
> Things fall apart; the centre cannot hold;
> Mere anarchy is loosed upon the world,
> The blood-dimmed tide is loosed, and everywhere
> The ceremony of innocence is drowned;
> The best lack all conviction, while the worst
> Are full of passionate intensity.
>
> Well, that was certainly true between the wars, and it damn nearly destroyed us. Is it true today? Not quite, because good people have convictions, rather too many of them. The trouble is, there is still no centre.[35]

It is a lack of confidence, plus cynicism and disillusionment, which is severely shaking the symbols of American civil religion. Fourteen million Americans are receiving welfare payments, and they are bitterly resented by the American workingman. In addition, a large portion of our working force finds itself unemployed or underemployed through no fault of its own; our current recession has disrupted the careers of thousands of our most highly trained and qualified personnel in technical fields, management, broadcasting, aerospace, medical research, and education. And the cybernetics revolution has only just begun. Can a nation long endure that is half workingmen and half subsidized nonworkers?

At this time, the President has imposed a price-wage freeze and other temporary measures to reverse the decline of our economy—remedies which will succeed only with the co-operation of the entire population. Once again we are called upon to make personal sacrifices for the national good. But for what? For the cause of freedom and liberty? For the sake of the American dream? Somehow the slogans "Support your dollar" and "End the balance of payments deficit" have little emotion power.

It is a dark hour for American civil religion. The traditions of the nation are being called into question. The young are estranged from the American Way of Life. Their elders are perplexed and fearful. The evolutionary optimism, rationalistic humanism, and messianic internationalism of the liberal heritage are in doubt. The insatiable consumerism and environmental shortsightedness upon which the Middle American Way depends have attracted a host of vehement critics. A bumper crop of cynics, seemingly enemies of everything Americans have cherished, appears to be the chief product of our burgeoning colleges and universities. *The usually tense but stable armistice between fervent revivalism and tolerant pluralism has been shattered.* Everywhere fundamentalism is on the march with its apocalyptic images of tomorrow and its socially indifferent gospel of personal redemption.

CONCLUSIONS

In his irritating but stimulating diatribe *Without Marx or Jesus,* Jean-François Revel declares:

> America has never had a state religion, either officially or otherwise. European wits who make fun of the endemic religiosity of America, as exemplified by the presence of Bibles in hotel rooms and the inscription "In God We Trust" on money, would do better to reflect on the consequences of a very important cultural fact: that no church of any kind has ever dominated, either by law or *de facto,* the moral, intellectual, artistic, or political life of that immense country. . . . It is true that the President of the United States swears his oath of office on the Bible, and that the President of France does not. The President of France, however, is not the one who is more free of confessional influence. And the same can be said if we compare the two countries . . . from the standpoint of freedom from religious influence in the classroom, in the newspaper office, and in the publishing house.[36]

Revel's contention that no organized denomination or church has ever dominated the culture or political life of the American people is unassailable. But the remainder of his argument is totally fallacious. Confessional influences may be present in France, but how seriously are they taken by French cultural, intellectual, and political leaders? The confessionalism of French Catholicism is overt, limited to special times and places, and easily avoided. Americans may lack an established church, but are scarcely free of religious influences in the political, intellectual, and cultural spheres of existence. (Where would a self-proclaimed atheist have a better chance of being elected to public office—in France or the United States?) America is a religious nation. All secular concerns are permeated by a religiosity which is complex, dialectic (i.e., essentially inconsistent), dynamic, and above all unavoidable. For the social, moral, and political decisions of Americans are motivated by the diverse interpretations of *what is important, what is good,* and *what is true* which we have discussed throughout these pages: *1*) the pietism of revivalistic Protestantism which finds its current expression in the preaching of Billy Graham, fundamentalism, and the so-called Jesus revolution; *2*) civil religion—sacrificial dedication to the traditions, values, and destiny of the nation; and *3*) the liberal heritage—an optimistic, progressivistic, and humanistic commitment to the transformation of America's social institutions.

The New Political Majority

Despite the deepening domestic and international crises can America survive? We believe the America sacralized by this three-stranded religiosity will survive. The resources for survival lie in the values of the religion of Middle America, values inherent in the words and deeds of Billy Graham. For Graham is the quintessential Middle American and he has built a constituency which reaches from the White House to Main Street, a following which today represents the broad center of the nation's population and values. Graham, who could be at home with Dwight Eisenhower of Kansas, Lyndon Johnson of Texas, Richard Nixon of California—is the man for this season, this trying time. For Graham, by combining religious assurance with the basic moderateness of traditional American concepts of morality and action, has put it all together.

Any analysis which perceives Billy Graham to be either the greatest revivalist of his time or White House "chaplain" falls short of defining his actual place in American society. Graham is today the leader of the politically decisive majority, the man who more consistently than anyone else articulates the aspirations and fears of the bulk of his fellow citizens. His vision of an America dedicated to God and committed to the ideals and dreams upon which the nation was founded is shared by Middle Americans. His description of America's problems, his rejection of extremism, his stress on the worth of the individual, his strong support of the work ethic, his suggestion that God has singled out America for special blessing and special responsibility elicit positive chords of response from an American majority which is deeply troubled but which desires to find a constructively moderate way out of the wilderness.

Graham, who through sincere introspection continues to regard himself as evangelist called to witness to the saving knowledge of Christ and the new birth, has transcended a purely theological ministry and has emerged as the spokesman not of preachers and Presidents but of the political views of the corporate majority of Americans.

The 1969 Gallup Poll indicated Middle America's response to the problems generated by the complexity of a rapidly changing society. The Gallup data suggests that this largest single group in American society is politically moderately conservative. The poll respondents oppose reparations being paid by church groups to blacks, favor stricter laws dealing with obscene literature, desire college officials to take a stronger stand on student disorders, uphold legislation making the possession of marijuana illegal. Such conservative but—it should be pointed out—non-extremist views coincide with the wish to have a politically conservative rather than a liberally oriented individual appointed to any new vacancies on the U.S. Supreme Court. When asked to list the *one* government program most wanted, the respondents favored action dealing with crime and law enforcement.

1969 Gallup Poll Results

	KEEP OR INCREASE	CUT
Anti-crime, law enforcement programs	22%	1%
Aid to education	19%	1%
Anti-poverty program	17%	6%
Medicaid	9%	2%
Air and water anti-pollution programs	8%	2%
Welfare and relief	8%	10%
Aid to cities	8%	5%
Subsidies to farmers	4%	7%
Financing Vietnam War	4%	18%
Building for highways	2%	9%
Space program	2%	39%

Richard L. Scammon and Ben J. Wattenberg note that while crime is number one on the list, there exists strong support for traditional social welfare programs (education, poverty, medical care). This indicates that voters in the seventies will be "conservative on the social issue, liberal on the bread and butter issue." They further suggest that "this attitudinal center today involves progressivism on economic issues and toughness on the social issue.[37]

The 1972 Presidential Race

Nixon's actions on both the domestic and international fronts have greatly enhanced his chances for success in 1972. It appears to the authors that the only type of Democratic candidate who could possibly defeat Nixon would have to begin with centrist appeal. This appeal, whether by a Protestant or Roman Catholic hopeful, must have some relation to the theological and social positions of Billy Graham. Unfortunately, Democratic candidates tend to have liberal, Eastern-based advisers on matters religious who automatically write off the fundamentalist potential. It is our belief that in 1972 a candidate who has not allied himself with the radical movement in America can build a coalition which includes all of the 1968 Democratic groupings as well as significant numbers of fundamentalists. In essence we do not concede the fundamentalist community to the Republicans and Nixon.

Today the Gallup Poll indicates that the pre-eminence of party affiliation has been replaced by the emergence of a new attitudinal center. The candidate who most effectively directs his energies toward the vast number of voters represented in this center will likely prevail. As Scammon and Wattenberg suggest, this is not only the soundest kind of political tactic, but also conforms to the dynamic of the democratic form of government active in America where "politicians are in business to represent the will of the majority of the people."[38] As Revel notes, "Despite so much talk about 'law and order,' all the great liberal legislative projects of the past few years have either come to a successful conclusion or are in the process of doing so." [39]

Expressing this conclusion in Graham–Middle America theological categories, the majority continue to identify with abstract principles in their understanding of the manner in which social problems are to be dealt with, while taking a decidedly more pragmatic view of problems which affect the immediate well-being of the individual. We believe the attitudinal center, reflected in the poll, is genuinely in tune with Graham's theological and social theory. We further suggest it is to this group that those seeking the Presidency in 1972 must basically appeal. Quite obviously President Nixon realizes this as his attempts to identify with Graham during the last several years clearly demonstrate. Indeed his Vietnam policy has been calculated to appeal to the moderate conservative who disavows the McIntire "destroy Hanoi" anti-communism while favoring "peace with honor." Nixon understands that the sacral America cannot be defeated on the battlefield and, as his new China position illustrates, he also knows that encounter in a controlled atmosphere where moderation rather than precipitousness will rule conforms to the image the decisive majority of Americans have concerning their nation, its traditions, values and achievements. Likewise, his new economic policy recognizes the Middle American necessity to regain philosophical optimism while experiencing an actual pocketbook advance. Richard Nixon has learned that politically and socially Billy Graham is "where it's at."

The more than thirty million evangelicals of voting age will not automatically "vote their faith" in the forthcoming Presidential election or in any other election. They are subject to the same pressures of personal need and socioeconomic realities as are other Americans. But they are *inclined* to distrust programs which assume that the condition of the individual or society can be improved by either new legislation or new clichés. They are *inclined* to distrust political figures who offer easy solutions to complex problems which can only be solved by disciplined effort and heroic self-sacrifice. They are dubious of the unrealistic utopianism which infects America's social, political, and international expectations. As Irving Kristol notes, American political leaders and the mass media have conditioned us to prefer high-flown utopian illusions to "realistic assessments of human beings, and to the world in which real human beings live." [40] Having surrendered the liberty to speak plainly, our leaders have lost the capacity to deal realistically with actual problems. Instead of seeing situations as they are, they have disciplined themselves to believe and take seriously their own empty rhetoric. Kristol writes:

> Every society needs ideals and self-criticism and some prophetic admonition. It needs these to correct its "natural" tendency toward smugness, inertia and parochial self-satisfaction. But when the countertendency toward insistent self-dissatisfaction becomes overwhelming, then such a society is in grave trouble. The capacity for contentment is atrophied. So is the willingness to see things as they really are, and then to improve them in a matter-of-fact way. We certainly do have it in our power to make improvements in the human estate. But to think we have it in our power to change people so as to make the human estate radically better than it is, radically different from what it is, and in very short order, is to assume that this generation of Americans can do what no other generation in all of human history could accomplish. American though I be, I cannot bring myself to accept this arrogant assumption. I think, rather, that by acting upon this assumption we shall surely end up making our world worse than it need have been.[41]

Fundamentalism and Our Present Condition

Because fundamentalists believe that only God can unravel the grotesque tangles and redeem the tragedies of human existence, they know better than to expect solutions where none are to be found. Thus, the disappearance of grounds for the perennial optimism of the American people has not had the fatal impact upon them that it has had upon the liberal religious and socio-political institutions of our national life. *The conservative Protestant always knew that America would end up just where it finds itself today.*

But the question remains whether fundamentalism has resources upon which the American people can draw in order to transcend the uneasiness and despair of the present. For the evangelical emphasis upon personal salvation has been responsible for indifference to political processes and social realities at a time when the indifference of our citizenry could be as destructive to all we cherish as the empty rhetoric of our habitual utopianism. Charles Lutz, a young Lutheran theologian, reminds us that "the values and presuppositions which the great bulk of Middle Americans hold were either given to them or supported by the teaching they received in their formation as Christians. Thus they have theological grounds for responding as they do in a time of rapid social and cultural change."[42] But will they respond? Will the evangelicals apply their numbers, their relative strength, their burgeoning influence, and the prestige which they have acquired through Billy Graham to undergird the values which they share with "the great bulk of Middle Americans"? Or will they allow their expectations of the impending end of the world to blind them to the demand which God makes of his children: "He has showed you, O man, what is good; and what does the Lord require of you but to do justice, and to love kindness, and to walk humbly with your God?" (Micah 6:8)

Revivalism and social reform have not always been opposed in the past nor need they be in the future. There is much in the faith of the evangelical community which encourages a spirit of Christian citizenship manifesting itself in compassion for others and a striving for justice. A few years ago, political scientist Murray S. Stedman, Jr., predicted:

> Those Protestant churches that have historically opposed social action [fundamentalist denominations and sects] will become even more prominent, while the social action-oriented denominations [the constituent members of the NCC] become less influential; the latter will probably face a period of relative

> decline in numbers. If sustained, these trends could mean increased Protestant political support for the status quo and thus a diminution in the over-all effectiveness of the Protestant churches as social critics.[43]

We would advise conservative Protestants to give Stedman's analysis their careful consideration. At the same time, we would question Stedman's assumption that the primary role of the church *vis-à-vis* society is that of critic. There can be no doubt that our society requires the prophetic judgment of the churches. However, social criticism without active involvement or commitment to substantive and creative alternatives is ultimately demoralizing. The great majority of Americans look to their churches and the clergy for much more than dispassionate criticism. They expect moral and spiritual leadership. They await hopeful images of their future and the future of America.

The Future of Protestantism

Does the growth of conservative Protestant influence mean the demise of mainline denominationalism? It would be naïve to suppose that these major institutions will vanish. Indeed Glock and Stark's projections of the long-range pattern of denominational switching warrant the belief that moderate and liberal churches will be the eventual beneficiaries of the conservative bonanza. But at present the fortunes of the mainline denominations and the various interchurch agencies are on the wane. Our analysis suggests that the fundamentalist advance in both influence and financial resources is directly related to those programs and policies of the mainline churches which have led to an accelerated disaffection by large numbers of communicants. The decline of the major denominations is not a healthy phenomenon since these groups have in the past exerted a positive and humane liberalizing force in our national life. Today a moderate liberalism commensurate with the flourishing moderate conservatism of Middle America would add balance to the manner in which our society reacts to the complex of problems which menace internal order and stability. The major denominations can respond constructively to the crises of the seventies by becoming less involved with social posturing and more interested in the inculcation of spiritual and moral values.

We strongly recommend that the major denominational and interdenominational bodies carefully evaluate all current social and political programs with the intention of eliminating those which in actual or potential terms increase polarization within American life. Indeed, we urge a one-year moratorium on such programming and a concomitant period of introspection and reflection by church leadership as to the proper societal direction Christians should take if they would be true to their fundamental faith perspectives. If such a course of action were pursued liberals and conservatives could jointly aid in enabling the nation to survive the contemporary crisis which threatens to erode vitally needed foundational principles and institutions. It is time that the zealous dedication of American fundamentalism and the social responsiveness of liberal Protestantism were joined together in support of a national heritage which is well worth saving. We hope that our words will encourage those who have not abandoned the heroic tasks of nation-building, those who seek, as Robert Kennedy so often said, "to tame the savage beast and make noble the way of man."

NOTES

1. Thomas Luckmann, *The Invisible Religion* (New York: The Macmillan Company, 1967), p. 37.
2. *Ibid.*
3. Bryan Wilson, *Religion in Secular Society* (Baltimore: Penguin Books, 1969), p. 112.
4. Will Herberg, *Protestant-Catholic-Jew* (New York: Anchor Books, 1960), p. 74.
5. *Ibid.*, p. 80.
6. "The Moon and Middle America," *Time,* August 1, 1969, pp. 10–11.
7. Will Herberg, *op. cit.*, pp. 78–79.
8. Robin M. Williams, Jr., *American Society. A Sociological Interpretation* (New York: Knopf Books, 1961), p. 417.

9. *The Philosophy of William James,* selected by Horace M. Kallen (New York: Modern Library, 1953), p. 305.
10. Robert Lee Miller, "Piety Along the Potomac," *The Reporter,* August 17, 1954.
11. Robert N. Bellah, "Civil Religion in America," in *Religion in America,* p. 3.
12. *Ideas and Self-Interest in America's Foreign Relations: The Great Transformation of the Twentieth Century* (Chicago: University of Chicago Press, 1953), pp. 444, 125. *Cf.* David Little, *American Foreign Policy & Moral Rhetoric* (New York: Council on Religion and International Affairs, 1969).
13. Bellah, *op. cit.,* p. 20.
14. *Ibid.*
15. *Ibid.,* p. 9.
16. *Ibid.*
17. *Ibid.,* p. 11.
18. William G. McLoughlin, "Is There a Third Force in Christendom?" in *Religion in America,* p. 48.
19. Gordon W. Allport, *The Individual and His Religion* (New York: Macmillan Paperbacks, 1960), p. 56.
20. Bellah, *op. cit.,* pp. 20–21.
21. Edward B. Fiske, "Praying With the President in the White House," *The New York Times Magazine,* August 8, 1971, pp. 14–15.
22. *Ibid.,* p. 20.
23. Quoted by Fiske, *ibid.,* p. 26.
24. *Ibid.,* p. 27.
25. *Ibid.,* p. 26.
26. *Ibid.,* p. 27.
27. Wilson, *op. cit.,* p. 121.
28. Kenneth Keniston, *The Uncommitted: Alienated Youth in American Society* (New York: Harcourt, Brace & Jovanovich, 1965), p. 224.
29. Calvin Redekop, "A Sociologist's Look at Religion in America," *Encounter,* Autumn 1968, p. 344.
30. *Ibid.*
31. Max Weber, *The Protestant Ethic and the Spirit of Capitalism* (New York: Charles Scribner's Sons, 1958).
32. "Kritische Bemerkungen zu den vorstehenden 'kritischen Beiträgen,'" *Archiv für Sozialwissenschaft,* Vol. XXV (1907), p. 248; cited by Reinhard Bendix, *Max Weber: An Intellectual Portrait* (New York: Doubleday Anchor Books, 1962), pp. 57–58.
33. *Ibid.,* p. 60.
34. Wilson, *op. cit.,* pp. 261–262.
35. Kenneth Clark, *Civilisation* (New York: Harper & Row, 1969), p. 347.
36. Jean-Françoís Revel, *Without Marx or Jesus: The New American Revolution Has Begun* (New York: Doubleday & Co., Inc., 1971), p. 217.
37. Richard M. Scammon and Ben Wattenberg, *The Real Majority* (New York: Coward, McCann, 1970), p. 73.
38. Scammon and Wattenberg, *op. cit.,* p. 79.
39. Revel, *op. cit.,* pp. 237–238.
40. Irving Kristol, "A Foolish American Ism—Utopianism," *The New York Times Magazine,* November 14, 1971, p. 31.

41. *Ibid.*, p. 103.
42. Charles Lutz, "Middle America: Theologically Formed," *The Christian Century*, March 18, 1970, p. 323.
43. Murray S. Stedman, *Religion and Politics in America* (New York: Harcourt, Brace & World, 1964), p. 9.

Index